Jackie Sheldon – Jackie was a corporate solicitor specialising in mergers and acquisitions. Jackie worked and trained at global law firm, Taylor Wessing, qualifying into their Projects department, working on large corporate transactions. She moved to the Northwest and continued to specialise in corporate transactions, working at Pannones followed by international law firm, Square, Sanders and Dempsey (then Hammonds).

Jackie is qualified to teach up to Masters level (receiving a Post Graduate Certificate in Professional Education), is a Fellow of the Higher Education Academy and has now been writing and delivering commercially relevant company law and related topics to both undergraduate and post graduates (including CPD and PSC) since 2006. She is also honoured to use her corporate legal knowledge in her position as a trustee/director, company secretary and vice chair for Mummy's Star – a unique charity in UK and Ireland.

Kate Shepherd – Prior to establishing her consultancy Kate Shepherd Associates in 2005, Kate qualified as a solicitor, and practised employment law at a senior level with a leading firm in the Midlands. Kate holds CIPD qualifications, a Post Graduate Diploma in Law and now runs a consultancy specialising in interactive online training delivery. Her team regularly design and deliver workshops to lawyers at both undergraduate and postgraduate level. Kate is also a published author and visiting lecturer for a number of Universities and Business Schools.

Advising Effectively on the Employment Aspects in a Corporate Transaction

A Practical Guide for Junior Lawyers

Advising Effectively on the Employment Aspects in a Corporate Transaction

A Practical Guide for Junior Lawyers

Jackie Sheldon
Solicitor, Director (*Maxlex Ventures Limited*),
Trustee/Director and Company Secretary (*Mummy's Star*)
LLB (Hons), PGDip (Law), FHEA, PGCPE

Kate Shepherd
Employer Lawyer, Trainer and Author
MD at Kate Shepherd Associates Ltd
LLB (Hons), F.Inst.LEx, PGDip (Law), Solicitor (Retired), CIPD qualified

Law Brief Publishing

Published 2021 by Law Brief Publishing, an imprint of Law Brief Publishing Ltd
30 The Parks
Minehead
Somerset
TA24 8BT

www.lawbriefpublishing.com

Paperback: 978-1-914608-02-5

PREFACE

Kate and Jackie have both been delivering training in relation to the corporate and employment issues in private company acquisitions for many years (including delivering joint courses together).

We noted that there was no text available analysing the key issues specifically aimed at addressing the needs of the employment team – appreciating that to advise effectively on the employment aspects of the transaction, an understanding of both the corporate and employment aspects are required. This text aims to address that need.

We would like to thank MBL Seminars for giving us both the opportunity to develop specialist supporting training workshops which sit alongside this textbook.

Stated law is believed to be correct and up to date as at 1 October 2021.

Jackie Sheldon
Kate Shepherd
October 2021

CONTENTS

CHAPTER ONE
INTRODUCTION

When advising on corporate transactions involving the sale of companies and businesses, regardless of the type of business being purchased, the amount of consideration being paid for the company or business and the parties involved, the key issues that need to be considered by the advisors will be the same.

The sellers will always aim for the highest value they can achieve (coupled with the lowest ongoing risks and obligations), whilst the buyer will be aiming for the lowest consideration possible (coupled with the smallest risks) whilst ensuring it acquires exactly what it thinks it is paying for.

This text will review a corporate transaction from the outset up to and including post completion elements. As the most important asset in many deals will be the people, the transaction must be structured properly to ensure the complexities are addressed and the advisors need a clear understanding of the issues inherent in a corporate transaction to be able to address their client's aims.

This text aims to consider all of the initial issues involved in structuring a transaction from a corporate perspective (including ensuring key company law concepts are addressed) and will then explore key contractual and statutory employment law concepts and their impact on the transaction.

A corporate transaction commonly refers to a private company acquisition and there are two key types of private company acquisition: a share sale and the sale of a business as a going concern. Each form will be analysed in depth in Chapter 3. It should also be noted that, as the aim of this text is to assist a junior practitioner, it also highlights points for use in practice throughout.

The text will not analyse the sale of individual assets and will not be looking at tax issues or any transaction outside of the United Kingdom. Where tax may be relevant, this text will highlight where tax input may be required.

CHAPTER TWO

FUNDAMENTALS OF EMPLOYMENT LAW

Introduction

Our first consideration when advising on the employment aspects in a corporate transaction should be the appreciation of some fundamental principles of employment law.

Often a corporate transaction will involve the ending of an employment relationship either by the transferor or the transferee. In this chapter we will consider what rights an individual employee has when their contract of employment is terminated with specific reflections on the issues that arise during a corporate transaction.

Rights on termination

Employees have specific employment law rights when their contract of employment comes to an end. First, we must consider the rights that arise under an employee's contract of employment. The second aspect are the rights that an employee has under various statutes, primarily the Employment Rights Act 1996 ("**ERA 1996**").

In order to access these rights, both under the contract of employment and the statutory rights under the ERA 1996, an employee must have been dismissed. This might sound an obvious point. However, there is a specific definition of dismissal under the ERA 1996 and an employee needs to be able to show that they have been dismissed in line with this definition in order to pursue a claim.

Section 95(1) ERA 1996 definitions of dismissal:

An employee is dismissed by their employer if:

- ***There is a positive act of dismissal by the employer:*** *The contract under which they are employed is terminated (with or without notice)*
- ***A fixed term contract comes to an end:*** *He is employed under a fixed term contract and that contract comes to an end without being renewed*
- ***There is a constructive dismissal:*** *The employee terminates the contract under which they are employed (with or without notice) due to the employer's conduct*

Practical tip: ensure you appreciate that during a commercial transaction employees have dismissal rights arising from their contract of employment as well as the ERA 1996.

Dismissal rights under the contract of employment

Wrongful dismissal

Wrongful dismissal arises when an employee has been dismissed in breach of the contract of employment. For example, when the employer has dismissed a member of staff and not given them sufficient notice of termination to which they are entitled under the contract of employment or failed to follow certain stages of a contractual disciplinary procedure.

The significance of wrongful dismissal is that an employee can bring a claim to an employment tribunal or through the courts without having to have the 2 years' continuous employment necessary for bringing a claim of unfair dismissal (see later section on unfair dismissal)

Enforcement

Wrongful dismissal claims are generally common law claims and as such are enforceable in the courts.

Wrongful dismissal claims can also be heard within the employment tribunal system, but, as tribunal awards are capped at £25,000, compensation from a county court or the High Court may be more beneficial to the claimant.

Remedies

The principle is that the employee should be put back in the financial position which they would have been in, had the contract been performed lawfully. Damages can potentially be quite high in some cases, for example where an employee is dismissed without notice and it is wrongful, a court can award compensation of the number of weeks' pay that would have been due. However, claimants are required to mitigate their loss, which may result in an award of compensation which is less than the face value of the breach of contract.

Practical tip: Generally, higher earning employees seeking to pursue wrongful dismissal claims will need to seek redress in the civil courts because of the £25,000 cap. Ensure you link up with your civil team to discuss this at an early stage.

Summary Dismissal

Summary dismissal is the dismissal of an employee without notice or pay in lieu of notice. It generally occurs as a result of an act of gross misconduct by the employee. In these circumstances the employee would not be entitled to receive any notice of termination and the employer would not have to pay in lieu of any notice.

An act of gross misconduct is so serious as to justify summary dismissal of an employee. The concept of gross misconduct relies on a repudiatory breach of the express or implied terms of the contract of employment through an employee's conduct.

A repudiatory breach is one which renders the whole contract broken. The breach is so serious that it relieves the employer from any further duties under the remainder of the contract.

Apart from a dismissal for gross misconduct, terminating the contract of employment without notice is likely to be a breach of the employment contract that could allow the employee to bring a claim of wrongful dismissal.

A fair process is required to be followed for summary dismissal. For acts of gross misconduct, it is normal to suspend the employee whilst an investigation is conducted, and the disciplinary meeting is arranged. Without this fair process, a tribunal could find the dismissal procedurally unfair.

Contractual benefits

Where an employee has been dismissed without due notice, they will also be entitled to the value of other contractual benefits that would have been available during that notice period, such as accrued holiday pay, company car (or equivalent allowance) and pension contributions.

Notice Periods

As we have outlined above, when an employee is dismissed, they are entitled to notice of that termination. The required notice period is the statutory amount, or the amount agreed in the contract of employment, whichever is longer.

An employee's required notice period must be given in their contract or written statement, or the statement must refer to the relevant legislation on notice periods.

To avoid disputes, most employers specify that notice must be given in writing so that a resignation date is transparent. In dismissal cases, an employer should specify a date of dismissal in order to be clear about when the notice of termination takes effect.

Statute requires that where an employer proposes to terminate employment, certain minimum periods of notice must be given by the employer to the employee.

Section 86(1) ERA 1996 requires:

(1) The notice required to be given by an employer to terminate the contract of employment of a person who has been continuously employed for one month or more—

(a) is not less than one week's notice if his period of continuous employment is less than two years,

(b) is not less than one week's notice for each year of continuous employment if his period of continuous employment is two years or more but less than twelve years, and

(c) is not less than twelve weeks' notice if his period of continuous employment is twelve years or more.

For the employee giving notice, the statutory requirement is less balanced:

Section 86(2) ERA 1996 states:

The notice required to be given by an employee who has been continuously employed for one month or more to terminate his contract of employment is not less than one week.

As you can see, an employee is only legally required to provide the employer with one week's notice of termination (after they have completed one month's service). This does not increase with an employee's length of service. That is why an employer will usually increase this minimum notice requirement in a contract of employment.

These requirements are the statutory minimum, and a contract of employment would usually contain express terms greater than the statutory minimum. For senior staff the periods of notice contained in a contract of employment are often much longer than the statutory amounts of notice, for example 6 months' notice of termination is not uncommon for directors and senior executives.

If an employee does not give the employer the correct notice of termination either under their contract or statutory notice, the employer can bring a claim against the employee for breach of the contract of employment. However, these types of claims are rare and not particularly practical, as the employer would need to show the business has been damaged in some way.

Pay in lieu of notice ("PILON")

A PILON clause enables the employer to terminate the contract early and lawfully.

Either the employer or the employee can waive its right to receive notice of termination of the contract of employment and accept a payment in lieu instead. If agreed, the parties can then treat the contract as terminated. An employer wanting to pay for notice in these circumstances should reserve the right to make a payment in lieu of notice in the contract of employment.

Garden Leave

When an employee leaves an employer, either because they have resigned or through dismissal, they have an implied right to continue attending their workplace during their notice period.

An employer might not always want an employee to continue working, perhaps because they might continue to have access to commercially sensitive information. In which case a garden leave clause can be inserted into the contract of employment which prevents the employee from having to attend work and in effect requiring the employee to remain at home during their notice period.

During this period of garden leave the employee is still entitled to be paid their full salary and benefits and remains bound by the terms of their contract of employment.

If an employer wants to put an employee on garden leave, there must be an express clause in the contract of employment.

Practical tip: ensure as a practitioner you appreciate the difference between garden leave and PILON clauses. Check your understanding on how these contractual clauses impact on the corporate transaction and the bargaining position of the parties

Rights on termination under the ERA 1996

Unfair dismissal

An employee has the statutory right not to be unfairly dismissed (**s94 (1) ERA 1996**).

Fair reasons for dismissal

An employer may fairly dismiss an employee provided that there is a fair reason for the dismissal. **Section 98 ERA** sets out potentially fair reasons for an employer to dismiss an employee. We will explore later that there are reasons which make a dismissal automatically unfair, but there are also reasons where the dismissal will usually be deemed a fair one. For there to be a fair dismissal an employer must show their reason for dismissing an employee was due to one of these fair reasons.

Once an employer has identified a fair reason for a dismissal, an employer must then follow a fair process.

Section 98 ERA sets out potentially fair reasons for an employer to dismiss which are:

i. conduct;
ii. capability;
iii. redundancy;
iv. statutory illegality; or
v. some other substantial reason (SOSR).

There are many reasons why an employer may want to dismiss an employee during a corporate transaction. For example, where there is a sale of a business as a going concern (which is explored in Chapter 3) and the purchaser does not want senior key employees from the transferor's business, if these employees are dismissed, this will be an automatic unfair dismissal as the only reason those individuals are being dismissed is because of the TUPE transfer (see Chapter 6).

Likewise, following a TUPE transfer if an employee is repeatedly late for work, or has unsatisfactory work performance; it will be reasonable for the transferee to dismiss for reasons relating to the employee's conduct provided that a fair disciplinary process has been followed.

Let's now explore each of these fair reasons in turn:

1. Conduct

Conduct, or more correctly misconduct, is one of the most common reasons for a dismissal. Dismissal for misconduct may be due to one occurrence of serious misconduct which is generally referred to as gross misconduct, or due to a series of smaller misdemeanours such as poor timekeeping, minor policy breaches or, for example, swearing. Conduct is often referred to in disciplinary procedures with examples of gross misconduct and more minor offences, so that employees are clear of acceptable standards of behaviour at work.

Before dismissing for misconduct, the employer should carry out a thorough investigation into the allegations, to be satisfied that on the balance of probabilities the employee committed the act(s).

The employer is expected to be fair and to inform the employee of what is being said against them by others, provide them with the evidence that is available and give them the opportunity to respond to the allegations. The means of achieving this will be discussed later.

The procedure used by the employer will be closely scrutinised by the employment tribunal, particularly how far the employer's procedure complies with or adopts the principles of the ACAS Code of Practice on Disciplinary and Grievance Procedures.

2. Capability

Capability concerns the employee's ability to perform the kind of work they are employed to do, having regard to 'skill, aptitude, health or any other physical or mental quality'. Dismissing an employee for capability therefore includes dismissal based on inability to do the job, failing to reach acceptable standards, underperformance in a role, as well as illness.

A tribunal will expect an employer to manage poor performance and illness in different ways. For example, it will be reasonable to warn an employee that they should improve their standard of work, it may not be reasonable to warn an employee "*to get well, or else*!"

Additionally, capability reasons should be clearly identified and managed properly. Employers need to consider whether or not an employee is inherently incapable ("cannot") or is not capable through laziness, negligence or perhaps sheer stubbornness ("will not"). These "will not" reasons are almost certainly going to fit more comfortably into a conduct reason rather than one of capability. There is often a fine line between cannot and will not, however an employer needs to identify at an early stage whether it is an issue of conduct or capability, as the two processes are managed very differently.

To dismiss for capability, an employer needs to use a progressive disciplinary procedure to encourage improved performance or attendance. The progressive approach; starting at the lowest stage of disciplinary action, offering training and support to help the employee meet agreed targets with further disciplinary action, ultimately leading to dismissal should the targets not be achieved.

The employer must produce evidence of poor performance, but need not prove that the employee was incapable of performing *all* their duties. The employer is expected to conduct a proper investigation or appraisal of the employee's performance, identify the problem, provide training, supervision and encouragement, monitor progress, give them a reasonable chance to improve and warn them of the consequences of not doing so.

Employers need to be careful to ensure performance improvement targets and timescales are reasonable and achievable. If an employee is set up to fail it is likely that a dismissal will be viewed as unfair.

In cases of long-term sickness or ill health, the employer should discuss matters with the employee as early as possible and continue contact throughout the absence. A medical investigation should be undertaken, and advice sought from medical experts on the employee's health. Alternative employment should also be considered.

Practical tip: ensure you appreciate the difference between conduct and capability, as both need to be managed in different ways either pre or post transfer. Conduct is generally thought to be within an employee's control and related to their behaviour. Capability is often not within an employee's control as they may not be *able* to do something/perform for reasons outside of their control e.g., long term illness.

3. **Redundancy**

Redundancy is a fair reason to dismiss an employee. The ERA 1996 also requires the employer to follow a fair procedure when managing redundancies. Even where the employer can show that redundancy is the reason for dismissal they must act reasonably.

Where a former employee brings a claim of unfair dismissal on the grounds of redundancy to an employment tribunal, an employer must show that redundancy was the fair reason for the dismissal. Even if redundancy is shown as the reason, if the employee shows they were chosen for a reason which is automatically unfair or there was a lack of consultation or warning, the employee will win their claim for unfair dismissal.

To establish redundancy as a fair reason an employer must show that a redundancy situation exists within the meaning of **s139 (1) ERA 1996.**

Section 139 ERA 1996:

> *(1) For the purposes of this Act an employee who is dismissed shall be taken to be dismissed by reason of redundancy if the dismissal is wholly or mainly attributable to—*
>
> *(a) the fact that his employer has ceased or intends to cease—*
>
> > *(i) to carry on the business for the purposes of which the employee was employed by him, or*
> > *(ii) to carry on that business in the place where the employee was so employed, or*

> *(b) the fact that the requirements of that business—*
>
> > *(i) for employees to carry out work of a particular kind, or*
> > *(ii) for employees to carry out work of a particular kind in the place where the employee was employed by the employer,*
>
> *have ceased or diminished or are expected to cease or diminish.*

Redundancy in itself is a valid reason for dismissing an employee and may be necessary in a corporate transaction. We will explore later the concept of ETO reasons under TUPE in Chapter 6, however it is important to stress that redundancy is a classic ETO reason. Put simply, it will entail a change in the workforce and can be relied upon as a defence by the dismissing employer.

Overview of a redundancy process

In addition, as with any other reason for dismissal, the tribunal needs to be satisfied that the employer has acted reasonably. The employer is required to:

- give adequate warning of impending redundancies;
- identify a pool of employees at risk of redundancy;
- consult with individuals who are affected;
- consult with unions and/ or employee representatives;
- seek volunteers for redundancy;
- fairly operate an objective selection procedure; and
- consider suitable alternative employment prior to dismissing.

The employer may also consider offering the right to appeal against any decision to dismiss.

Redundancy Consultation

Individual consultation

If an employer is making fewer than 20 employees redundant there is a clear process which should be followed which includes meeting with the affected employee on a one-to-one basis and discussing the redundancy with them.

It should be explained to the employee that the employer is considering making the employee's job redundant and an explanation given of the reasons why the particular post is the one to be selected. At this stage no decision has yet been made and the employee should be given a reasonable amount of time to consider their position and to make suggestions. What is a reasonable period of time is not defined in law, although typically this could be between two and four weeks for a small employer.

A further meeting should be held to hear any proposals put forward by an employee and at which the final decision can be taken; and it is good practice to offer the right to appeal and to hold an appeal hearing, if the employee wishes to appeal against the decision to make them redundant.

Collective consultation with trade unions and/or employee representatives

Under **s188 Trade Union and Labour Relations (Consolidation) Act 1992 ("TULR(C)A) 1992")** where redundancies are proposed which affect between 20 and 99 employees at one establishment within a 90-day period, employers are under a *statutory* duty to consult with appropriate representatives of employees for a minimum of 30 days.

Where 100 or more employees are affected, a minimum 45 day consultation period with any appropriate representatives is required.

If there is a recognised trade union the consultation must be with trade union representatives.

Collective consultation must begin in good time and must include ways of avoiding or reducing the redundancies and mitigating the consequences of redundancies.

Consultation should include:

- the reasons for the redundancies;

- the numbers and descriptions of jobs it is proposed to make redundant;
- the total number of employees in the organisation where the redundancies are occurring;
- the method of carrying out the redundancies, including the selection criteria;
- how redundancy pay will be calculated; and
- any proposals for reducing or avoiding the redundancies and for mitigating or reducing their consequences.

Under the provisions of the **TULR(C)A 1992**, employers are also required to notify the Secretary of State of redundancies of 20 or more employees on one site.

Through consultation, the employer is not obliged to accept contrary views and does not have to accept the employee's views or proposals. However, they must properly consider them and should be able to evidence that they listened and considered the employee's views before reaching a final decision.

In collective redundancy situations, the failure to consult unions or employee representatives will generally render a dismissal as unfair. Even where collective consultation takes place, there is also the requirement for employers to consult with employees individually.

> Practical tip: often employers want to use redundancy as a reason for dismissing to "soften the blow" to the employee, perhaps to mask other underlying performance issues. Ensure that if your client is using redundancy as a fair reason for a dismissal, that it is a genuine redundancy situation and ensure they follow a fair redundancy process.

Redundancy pay

Statutory redundancy pay

Employees who have two years' service with an employer are entitled to receive a statutory redundancy payment ("**SRP**") if they are made redundant. SRP is calculated on the basis of a person's age and length of service.
To receive SRP, an individual must:

- be an employee, i.e., partners, casual workers, agency workers, the self-employed and directors not working under a contract of employment do not qualify;
- have at least two years' continuous service; and
- have been dismissed.

SRP is based on:

- the employee's age;
- the employee's amount of continuous service - up to a maximum of 20 years; and
- the employee's weekly pay - up to a statutory limit which is reviewed by the government from time to time.

An employee has six months from the date their employment ended to make a claim for payment to an employment tribunal where either:

i. The employee disagrees with the amount of the payment; or
ii. The employer fails to make any SRP.

> Practical tip: save a statutory redundancy payment calculator to your desktop, where you can input an employee's age, length of service and rate of pay. There are various websites with access e.g.: https://www.gov.uk/calculate-employee-redundancy-pay.

Contractual enhanced redundancy pay

As you can see from the above statutory redundancy payment calculations, the rates are relatively low. Often employers will enhance or top up the statutory redundancy payment. For example, rather than applying the statutory limit (which at the time of writing is £544 - April 2021-22) the employer would calculate an enhanced redundancy payment based on the employee's full pay rather than applying the statutory cap.

Therefore, careful consideration needs to be given to the contractual terms, which should be highlighted during the due diligence process and through the employee liability information (see Chapter 6 below).

4. Statutory Illegality

An employer may dismiss an employee in circumstances where their continued employment would be illegal. For example, if a bus driver is disqualified from driving, they may be fairly dismissed as they are employed solely to drive, and to allow them to continue to drive would be illegal. Similarly, to dismiss an employee who is not permitted to work legally in the UK is a potentially fair reason for dismissal on the grounds of statutory illegality.

In the case of a driving ban, before dismissing the employee, an employer should first consider the likely duration of the ban; whether the ban affects all or part of the employee's work; and whether the employee can be redeployed. In other words, if driving is only part of an employee's job and/or the employer's business has scope to provide alternative tasks that could be allocated, then it may be unfair to dismiss in those circumstances. However, if driving duties comprise **all** of the employee's duties then in such circumstances, if other work is not available, it may be fair to dismiss.

5. Some other substantial reason ("SOSR")

A SOSR dismissal almost seems to be a "catch all" reason, in that if the reason does not fall within any of the other four reasons it may be caught by this one. Case law shows a variety of different situations that fall within SOSR, the two most common situations that arise are for business needs and pressure from third parties. In a corporate transaction, SOSR is often used as a fair reason, particularly when terminating a contract of employment and reengaging on fresh terms and conditions. The dismissal in these circumstances would be for SOSR.

There are a number of cases where a tribunal has found an employer could justify a dismissal for SOSR. The fairness of a dismissal for SOSR will depend on whether, in the circumstances (including the size and administrative resources of the business), the employer had acted reasonably or unreasonably in treating that reason as a legitimate reason for dismissing the employee in question (see **Treganowan v Robert Knee & Company Limited** [1975] **IRLR**

247, Scott Packing and Warehousing Co Ltd v Paterson [1978] and **Skyrail Oceanic Limited t/a Cosmos Tours v Coleman** [1978] **IRLR 226**).

Eligibility to pursue a claim of unfair dismissal

To be eligible to present a complaint of unfair dismissal to an Employment Tribunal, an individual must be an employee and have been continuously employed for at least two years of employment (**s108 ERA 1996**).

Automatic unfair reasons

There are a number of automatically unfair reasons for dismissal. If a dismissal falls within one of these automatic unfair dismissal reasons, it means that an employee does not have to have two years' continuous service with an employer to be able to bring a claim of unfair dismissal (except in TUPE cases). In such cases the dismissal will be deemed to be automatically unfair. This means that once the tribunal has established that the reason for the dismissal falls under one of these heads, it will not have to go on to consider the reasonableness of the decision under s98(4) ERA 1996.

There are a number of special cases where the normal rules relating to unfair dismissal are varied and one of these is where an employee is dismissed prior to, or immediately following, the transfer of a business under TUPE. However, it must be stressed that whilst this is referred to as an automatic unfair dismissal under TUPE, an employee still needs to have 2 years' service in order to qualify for the right not to be unfairly dismissed.

Other automatic unfair dismissal reasons (not requiring 2 years' service include dismissal for pregnancy or maternity related reasons, dismissal for undertaking a statutory duty (e.g., jury service) and dismissal for whistleblowing under the Public Interest Disclosure Act 1998.

Remedies for unfair dismissal

There are three main remedies available to employees who are found to have been unfairly dismissed.

- Reinstatement - the reversal of the dismissal decision so the employee gets their old job back.
- Re-engagement - a claimant does not return to their previous role, but they return to a different job with the employer.

- Compensation.

Compensation for unfair dismissal

Given that orders for reinstatement or re-engagement are made in fewer than 1% of cases, the main remedy for unfair dismissal is financial compensation. This is made up of two key elements.

Basic award

The basic award is to compensate the employee for the loss of their job. It is calculated in exactly the same way as a statutory redundancy payment (see above) and is based on a person's age and length of service as follows:

- 1/2 a week's pay for each year worked before 22nd birthday;
- 1 week's pay for each year worked between 22nd and 41st birthday;
- 1 1/2 week's pay for each year worked after 41st birthday.

The above is subject to a statutory maximum weekly rate which is reviewed annually and a maximum of 20 years' service. In addition, the award can be reduced for:

1 conduct;
2 unreasonable refusal of an offer of reinstatement;
3 any redundancy pay received;
4 any ex-gratia payment.

Compensatory award

The compensatory award is to compensate the employee for the loss they have suffered as a result of the dismissal. The tribunal will take into account a variety of factors when assessing compensation under this heading including loss of earnings, loss of benefits, expenses in looking for work, loss of pension rights and loss of employment protection (**s123 ERA 1996**).

Essentially the purpose of the compensatory award is to compensate the employee for their financial loss. It is not aimed at penalising the employer, but to put right the employee's loss. An award may be reduced by any earnings since the dismissal or any social security benefits received and an unfair dismissal claimant has a duty to try to find another job as quickly as possible in order to 'mitigate their loss'.

The tribunal has the power to award compensation for future loss; that is loss which has not occurred at the date of the hearing. Future loss is at the discretion of the tribunal and will depend largely on the employee's prospects for securing another post quickly e.g., it will be more difficult to find another role if the employee only has particular sector experience or lives in a remote location.

In an unfair dismissal claim the limit on the compensatory award shall be the lower of a set amount (currently **£89,493 April 2021/2**) and the product of 52 multiplied by a week's pay of the employee concerned.

Constructive Dismissal

Put simply, constructive dismissal arises when an employee resigns and feels that they have no option but to do so because of the employer's unreasonable behaviour. Generally, an employer's behaviour needs to be so unreasonable as to fundamentally breach the contract of employment.

Examples of constructive dismissal include:

- demoting an employee without good reason;
- reducing an employee's pay without a good reason;
- changing someone's job responsibilities without consulting with them; and
- failing to pay salary and/or benefits to an employee.

The statutory definition of constructive dismissal is found in **s95(1)(c) ERA 1996** which provides:

> " (1) An employee is dismissed by his employer if
>
> (c) the employee terminates the contract under which he is employed (with or without notice) in circumstances in which he is entitled to terminate it without notice by reason of the employer's conduct."

It does not automatically follow that because the employer is in breach of contract that the constructive dismissal is *unfair* (see ***Hall v Lodge [1977] IRLIB***

76). As we have outlined above for a dismissal to be fair, the employer must have a fair reason and also act reasonably in all the circumstances.

If the employer is guilty of conduct which is a significant breach going to the root of the contract of employment, or which shows that it no longer intends to be bound by one or more of the essential terms of the contract, then it is in *repudiatory breach* of contract.

The employee may choose to treat any further performance of the contract as discharged. In other words, the contract is broken, and the parties are no longer bound by any other part of it.

For constructive dismissal, two elements are therefore needed:

- Repudiatory conduct on the part of the employer. This may be an actual or anticipated breach, but it must be sufficiently fundamental to justify the employee resigning. The breach can be a breach of an explicit term of the contract, or a breach of the implied term of trust and confidence; and

- A decision by the employee not to accept the breach and treat the contract as at an end. The employee must act in response to the breach and must not delay too long or else it may be deemed that the employee has accepted the breach.

The "last straw" principle

Under this principle, an employee can resign in response to a series of breaches of contract or a course of conduct by their employer which, taken cumulatively, amounts to a breach of the implied term of trust and confidence. It is called the last straw principle because often the final incident in the chain is in itself insubstantial, but is nonetheless sufficient to render the whole series of incidents as a breach of the implied term. The case of ***London Borough of Waltham Forest v Omilaju [2004] EWCA Civ 1493*** is a useful illustration of the "last straw" principle and the factors the Court of Appeal took into consideration.

Summary

In this chapter we've considered a number of key principles in employment law that the parties need to take into account throughout a corporate transaction. Our next chapter explores the corporate aspects of a transaction.

CHAPTER THREE

UNDERSTANDING THE CORPORATE ASPECTS OF A TRANSACTION

What is a corporate transaction?

When advising in relation to corporate transactions, it helps to have an overview of what is going on. Take the time to draw yourself a diagram of the relevant parties and keep it to hand when you are reviewing any documentation.

The term "transaction" was introduced in Chapter 1. A "corporate transaction" is a wide term but, in this context, refers to the sale and purchase of the shares of a company (or the assets of a business run by a company). We will look at the differences between these two types of transactions below. However, just as it was important in Chapter 2 to review some fundamental principles of employment law, as both transactions involve '*a company*' it is also useful to briefly review what a company is.

A company is a separate legal person. It can own its own assets, employ employees, enter into contracts and sue or be sued. It is registered at Companies House (where you can carry out a free search to find out a variety of information about the company).

As a company is inanimate, it needs individuals to both own it and run it. They may in fact be the same people, but it is important to be clear on their differing roles. The owners of the company are known as members (or shareholders), and the directors are the day-to-day managers of the company.

The corporate transaction will be taking place as the owners of the company (the shareholders) will have decided to sell the shares in their company (or the assets of the business that the company runs).

> Practical tip: Draw a diagram identifying all the parties (including the target company or business, the buyer(s) and the seller(s) and refer to it whenever you are advising on the transaction.

Methods of sale

There are usually two methods of selling a private company: by way of private treaty sale or by way of auction.

A private treaty sale is a transaction between a buyer and a seller. It is this form of sale we will be addressing throughout this book. In practice it may be that the parties already know each other, or the seller actively seeks a purchaser for the target company or business, or the buyer is looking for a company or a business to buy.

If the seller thinks the acquisition may be popular and there is the potential that more than one buyer could be found, it may wish to have an auction sale instead of a private treaty sale. An auction in this context is not a traditional auction by way of an auctioneer armed with a gavel. It is simply where several bidders are all interested in purchasing the target company or business. By virtue of the fact several bidders are all interested, there is a variation of the steps in the acquisition process (including differing preliminary documentation), with the potential that the seller may achieve a higher asking price than they would have achieved in negotiations with just one buyer.

This book will only address a private treaty sale and we will not be looking at auctions in any further detail.

Types of acquisition (share sales and business sales)

In practice, this is the most important issue to understand when assisting on an acquisition. It must be the first question you ask your supervisor – "*what kind of transaction are we advising on*?" Many supervisors assume the team is clear on the structure – do not be afraid to ask.

Whether the transaction is structured as a share sale or the sale of a business has an overarching impact on the whole transaction, therefore it is fundamental to be clear on the differences between the two types of acquisition, including the legal reasons behind the choice.

Practical tips:

- Ask at the outset what kind of deal you are advising on: share sale or business sale?
- Be clear who you are acting for – the buyer(s) or the seller(s).

Share sale

In a share sale, the only item being sold are the shares in the target company (the "**Target**"). Nothing else changes. If the buyer is purchasing all the shares in the Target, the only thing that is being altered is the ownership of the Target – it was owned by the seller(s) prior to completion of the acquisition, and it will be owned by the buyer after completion of the transaction.

To the outside world, the Target remains the same the day before completion of the transaction as the day after completion – it still owns all of the assets (and retains all of the liabilities) that it had prior to the transaction and carries out the same business. The only thing that has changed are the owners (the shareholders of the Target).

The shareholders of the Target are known as the "**Seller**(s)" – these are often either individuals, companies, or a combination of both.

Real life example: PepsiCo acquired the entire issued share capital of SodaStream International Ltd in 2019. The press announcement welcomed SodaStream to the PepsiCo family, illustrating beautifully that nothing changes other than the parent/owner (the shareholders) of the Target.

> Practical tip: Be clear on what form the Seller(s) are – are they individuals or corporate entities? This is important for the tax team to be aware of from the outset.

Sale of a business

When a business sale is referred to in the context of a private acquisition, the parties are usually referring to the sale of a business as a going concern. You often hear the term "**TOGC**" in practice – this stands for Transfer of a Going Concern.

What this means is that the buyer is purchasing each of the individual assets that they need to carry out the business they wish to purchase (such as land, plant, machinery, contracts, intellectual property, goodwill etc.). After completion of the transaction, the buyer will run the business and the Seller (the trading company) continues to exist – it will continue to retain any assets the buyer chose to leave behind, retain any liabilities and it will also contain the monies paid by the buyer to the Seller in consideration for the business – in practice, it is considered to be a "cash shell" as it is a (relatively) empty company other than the consideration received for the business. If the Seller only owned and operated the business that was sold, the Seller will not be continuing to trade after completion.

Real life example: In February 2021, Asos purchased Topshop and Miss Selfridge for £330 million. Asos did not wish to acquire any warehouses or distribution centres. The assets it chose to purchase included the brands and current and future stock.

For this text, when discussing an asset or business sale, we will assume that the buyer wishes to carry out a TOGC (i.e., the buyer will carry out the business being acquired after completion of the transaction). This book will not look at the sale and purchase of individual assets.

> Practical tip: When drawing the diagram of the parties, ensure you are clear on the identity of the Seller(s). On a share sale, this will be the shareholders of the Target. On the sale of a business as a going concern, it is the trading company itself that will be Seller (as it is selling all its individual assets to the buyer).

<u>Factors impacting on choice of acquisition – the buyer's perspective</u>

It may be over simplistic to assert that buyers generally prefer business sales and Seller(s) prefer share sales.

However, the key benefit to the buyer on a business sale is that it can cherry pick the assets it wishes to purchase (and leave behind any assets it does not want together with any liabilities of the trading company). As noted above in relation to the Asos example, the buyer did not want to acquire any properties (as Asos did not intend to keep any of the stores open because their business model is not a "store business" – they are an online retailer) so an asset sale was more suitable, enabling them to purchase the brands but leave the properties behind.

There are several drawbacks for the buyer to the sale of a business – it can be disruptive and there is no continuity (for example, the day before completion the business is run by the Seller(s) and the day after completion of the transaction, the buyer has taken over).

There can also be delay or uncertainty in the acquisition, as every individual asset being acquired must be transferred from the Seller(s) to the buyer. This may include consents from third parties being obtained (which are never guaranteed).

It is also vital that every asset that is required by the business is transferred. Some assets can be physically transferred (such as stock) but other assets will need additional documentation dealing with the transfer (such as transferring title of land) or assigning intellectual property.

You will also see in Chapter 6 that one key issue in relation to the sale of a business is that TUPE applies (and therefore will require significant additional input in relation to the employee issues of the relevant transaction) – Chapter 6 will focus on these implications.

It is a long-standing principle that TUPE does not apply in relation to the sale of shares.

In relation to a share sale, continuity is the main benefit to a buyer (as nothing changes in relation to the Target) and it is much simpler to effect – as noted above with an asset sale, every asset must be individually transferred. On a share sale, the only item to be transferred are the shares in the Target (therefore a stock transfer form (also sometimes referred to as Form J30) per shareholder is the only legal requirement necessary to transfer the shares).

Tax may also be favourable to the buyer on a share sale. The buyer will pay stamp duty on the sale of shares (currently 0.5% at the time of writing) for any sale of £1,000 or over. If the buyer wanted to buy the assets of a business (which included property), the buyer would be required to pay stamp duty land tax if the property or land is over a certain price. This stamp duty land tax at the time of writing is currently at a higher rate than the rate of stamp duty on shares.

The main drawback for the buyer on a share sale is that it is acquiring the whole of the Target, including any hidden liabilities. Any issues that may be lurking in the Target are an indirect concern to the buyer as it can impact on the value of the Target – it goes back to the fundamental difference between the two forms of sale – on a share sale, the buyer acquires the Target as a whole. As a result, the pre contract investigations into the Target (see Chapter 5) need to be significantly deeper on a share sale, to ensure the buyer is fully aware of any hidden issues and is then able to negotiate appropriate contractual protections to address these issues and risks (see Chapter 9).

Factors impacting on choice of acquisition – the Seller's perspective

As noted, Seller(s) generally prefer share sales for two reasons.

The first is that they get a clean break from the Target – the whole of the Target is sold as the Seller is selling all of the shares in the Target to the buyer (although contractual liabilities to the buyer under the sale and purchase agreement do remain). They also receive the consideration directly as the buyer purchases the shares from the Seller(s) and pays the consideration directly to the Seller(s).

The second reason is the potential tax exemptions and reliefs potentially available to the Seller(s) on a share sale. Examples of these at the time of writing include Substantial Shareholding Exemption available to corporate Seller(s) who satisfy the applicable tests (and results in no corporation tax payable on the consideration received for the transaction) or Business Asset Disposal Relief or Investors Relief available to individual Seller(s) who satisfy the applicable tests (and in each case, result in reducing the individuals applicable rate of Capital Gains Tax payable on the consideration received for the transaction (up to a specified lifetime limit).

TAX FLAG: tax advice is outside the scope of this text and must be taken in relation to the appropriate sale structure/potential exemptions and reliefs available to the clients. This resulting tax advice is usually a driving reason for the choice of sale structure.

5 key stages of a typical acquisition

Whether the sale is a share sale or sale of a business as a going concern, the key stages of a typical private acquisition by way of private treaty sale remain the same.

Stage 1 – Preliminary documentation / pre-contract stage

We will look at the preliminary documentation you would expect in a private treaty sale in Chapter 4.

In addition to the preliminary documentation, the pre-contract stage also includes the buyer conducting pre-contract investigations into the Target or the business it wishes to purchase – this is known as due diligence, and we will look at this in Chapter 5.

Stage 2 – Sale and Purchase Agreement / contract stage

We will look at this key document in Chapter 8.

Stage 3 – Exchange

Stage 3 may not be required as a stand-alone stage. Ideally, there will be a simultaneous exchange (which is where the sale and purchase agreement is signed) and completion (see Stage 4 below). However, there are often occasions where it is necessary for there to be a gap between the two stages. This is usually where conditions are required to be complied with (known as conditions precedent), which can include issues such as obtaining competition clearance, HMRC or other regulatory clearance, shareholder approval or landlord consent.

The Seller(s) will wish to ensure the buyer is bound to purchase the Target or business once the conditions are satisfied and the buyer will wish to ensure that there are no material adverse changes in the Target or the business since exchange. We will explore this in more detail in Chapter 10.

Stage 4 – Completion

This is where the title to the shares is transferred to the buyer on a share sale or the assets on a business sale in exchange for the buyer paying the consideration to the Seller. We will look at this process in Chapter 10.

Stage 5 – Post Completion

Once the sale and purchase agreement has been exchanged and completion has taken place (including monies paid), the job (particularly for the junior assistant in the team) does not end there. There are hugely important formalities that must be complied with to ensure that legal title to the shares /assets passes to the buyer; including ensuring any stamp taxes are paid within the correct time limits, any securities are registered, and other appropriate filings are made at Companies House within the correct time limits and any post completion work that is required to ensure the business sold is assimilated into the buyer's group. This is discussed in more detail in Chapter 10 and employment post completion issues are analysed separately in Chapter 11.

CHAPTER FOUR

PRE-CONTRACTUAL DOCUMENTATION

Stage 1 – preliminary documentation

There are two key preliminary documents you would expect to see at the outset of a private treaty sale – the first is a confidentiality agreement and the second is the heads of terms. We will look at each of these in turn.

Confidentiality agreement

This is often also known as an NDA (or non-disclosure agreement). This will usually be a short, non-contentious agreement between the buyer and the Seller(s) where the buyer agrees to keep any information about the Target (and the very fact of the proposed transaction) confidential. It will also agree to procure its advisors will also comply with the terms of the confidentiality agreement. It will also deal with how information should be destroyed or returned in the event the transaction fails to complete (and what happens in the event of a breach).

This is a vital document in a transaction, as if the fact the transaction is proposed leaks to the public, it can impact on the value of the transaction (and the Target or business as a whole may be devalued) as clients may choose to go elsewhere, staff morale can be damaged and if the sale does not complete, the Seller(s) may be left with a damaged Target or business.

The confidentiality agreement may last for several years or indefinitely (and ideally, the Target should be made a party to ensure it can enforce the obligations of the contract, as it will be the Target that suffers loss in the event of a breach). If the Target is not going to be made a party, it is important to ensure the boilerplate clause relating to the Contracts (Rights of Third Parties) Act 1999 is amended to state that the Target is to benefit from the obligations in the confidentiality agreement.

This confidentiality agreement should be signed before any information at all is provided to the prospective buyer. However, it should be clear that the commercial reality is such that a confidentiality agreement cannot prevent damage from taking place (for example, what happens if an unscrupulous buyer is only feigning interest in the corporate transaction to gain access to the confidential information of a competitor?).

For this reason, thought should also be given to how much information is provided at the outset of the transaction and whether due diligence should be conducted in staggered phases (see Chapter 5).

Practical tip: When drafting the confidentiality agreement, remember to check the following:

- Parties (consider including the Target/check Contracts (Rights of Third Parties) clause to ensure Target can enforce agreement)
- Length of time agreement lasts for
- Definition of confidential information (ensure it includes the very fact of the proposed sale as well as all the Target's confidential information)
- Obligation not to disclose the confidential information (other than to the authorised parties and ensure these parties are defined/buyer procures their compliance)
- Obligations to return or destroy information if transaction does not proceed
- Consequences for breach

Heads of terms

This is an optional document and has a wide variety of names. It is often called "HoT", "Memorandum of Understanding", "MOU" or "Term Sheet". They are all the same thing – it is a simple summary of the basic commercial terms in relation to the transaction and is merely (for the most part) an expression of intention.

This document is a useful aid to drafting the sale and purchase agreement and can also carry moral force (for example, you are free to negotiate away from any commercial items that have been agreed in the heads of terms (such as price), but it is commercially more difficult, unless you have a reason for your change in position, i.e. a liability has been discovered that reduces the value of the Target).

The majority of the clauses in the heads of terms are not legally binding (such as parties, consideration proposed and draft timetable).

However, some clauses can be expressed to be legally binding, such as exclusivity, costs, law and jurisdiction and confidentiality (assuming a separate NDA has not been entered – see above). Ideally, the confidentiality agreement will be signed prior to the heads of terms, but if this is not the case, the confidentiality clause must be expressed to be legally binding, and the same issues discussed above should be included in the heads of terms.

Exclusivity is the other key item to be considered including in the heads of terms. The buyer does not want to spend time (and money) investigating the Target and being involved in potentially lengthy negotiations with the Seller(s), only to discover that the Seller(s) have sold the Target to another bidder.

The buyer cannot force the Seller to maintain negotiations them until a deal is achieved (this is known as a 'lock in' and would be unenforceable) – essentially the buyer cannot make the Seller negotiate with them.

However, it is possible to "lock out" the Seller(s) from negotiating with other parties for a defined period. This gives the buyer a set period to investigate the Target and negotiate without the additional pressure of competing with other buyers. This exclusivity clause is enforceable if it is drafted correctly, (including consideration is provided for the obligation and it is drafted as a fixed and certain period of time to ensure it is not void for uncertainty). Remedies for breach can be damages for breach of contract or an injunction.

> Practical tip: When drafting/checking a lock out, ensure there is consideration for entering into the lock out (or it is signed as a deed in lieu of consideration) and that the exclusivity period is a set duration.

CHAPTER FIVE
DUE DILIGENCE

Purpose

Due diligence is usually carried out by the buyer because of the Latin phrase "*caveat emptor*" (which means "let the buyer beware"). It essentially means that the buyer is purchasing the Target or business at its own risk. It applies to both forms of acquisition; either the buyer is purchasing the whole Target (including any hidden liabilities), or they are buying the business as a going concern.

In either structure, the buyer will need reassurance that they are purchasing what they think they are buying, that they will get proper title to the assets that they are acquiring (which would be the shares on a share sale or the assets of the business on an asset sale), and what the extent of the liabilities they will either indirectly acquire on a share sale, or that they may be asked to acquire on an asset sale (or that they wish to negotiate to exclude from the acquisition).

The issues discovered during due diligence will impact on the negotiations, the protections the buyer may seek in the documentation and additional items that may be required as part of the transaction process.

A key point to remember is that the due diligence **must** be more detailed on a share sale than on a business sale. This goes to the root of the differences between the two transactions – on a share sale, the buyer is acquiring the entire Target (including its hidden liabilities). On the sale of a business as a going concern, the due diligence can be limited to the specific assets and liabilities that the buyer has chosen to purchase together with the employee issues (see Chapter 6 below).

Types and scope of due diligence

Types

In this text, we are considering legal due diligence (which is what the buyer's solicitors will be undertaking). It is worth bearing in mind that this exercise is usually not carried out in isolation and other types of due diligence may be conducted too (such as commercial due diligence (which can include environmental due diligence, insurance, market research, information technology etc.) and financial due diligence.

This text is only discussing buyer legal due diligence, but it is important to mention vendor due diligence. Vendor due diligence is where the Seller provides a due diligence report to the bidders on an auction. This saves the potential buyers from having to carry out the due diligence themselves (although they do have access to the information that the report is based upon).

As noted above, we are focusing on a private treaty sale which would be unlikely to utilise vendor due diligence. It is more commonly seen on an auction sale, where the due diligence report would be made available to a number of different bidders.

Scope

This is a key question when undertaking due diligence – what the scope of your review is i.e., what are you reviewing and what are you not considering/not reviewing.

It may be that the client has given specific instructions about issues you have been told to ignore/possible financial thresholds or even how long they wish you to spend conducting the due diligence.

This should all be set out clearly in the client care/engagement letter (including limiting your firms' liability for the due diligence). Ensure that you ask to read this letter/review the scope of the due diligence exercise before starting the process.

It should be noted that this text looks at corporate/commercial and employee issues but there are many other areas of due diligence that will need review depending on the nature of the Target/business that is being acquired such as banking, property, environmental, insurance, intellectual property, information technology, data protection, bribery and modern slavery for example.

<u>Examples of key corporate/commercial issues</u>

Change of control/prohibition on assignment

On a share sale, as nothing changes other than the owner of the shares, there may be key contracts between the Target and third parties that contain change of control provisions. These provisions allow the third parties to the contract to terminate the contract in the event of a change in control of the Target (i.e., completion of the share sale). These clauses are usually included if the third party is concerned about the change of ownership of the Target (for example, what happens if the Target is to be sold to their competitor).

If the transaction is structured as a business sale, change of control is not an issue but instead, it needs to be ascertained if there are key contracts that contain prohibition on assignment?

In either circumstance, if these are issues in your transaction, the third party will need to consent to the transaction which will need to be factored into the completion timetable (and additional documentation will need to be prepared to deal with this). This will either be a waiver of change of control rights on a share sale or consent to assignment (or a novation or negotiation of a fresh contract) in relation to a business sale. See Chapter 8 for more information on the transfer of contracts on an asset sale.

Consents/licences/clearances

The items discovered during the due diligence process will need to be factored into completion including the third-party consents noted above in relation to change of control/prohibition on assignment. In addition, other consents may be required, which could include regulatory consent, HMRC clearance, competition clearance, shareholder consent etc.

The key is that you are analysing the information provided by the Seller(s) to ascertain any possible impact on your client and the transaction itself.

<u>Other considerations</u>

The buyer will want to know who the key clients are and if there are any other existing contractual liabilities that impact on the acquisition. These considerations vary depending on what is being purchased.

<u>Example of issues to check in a key commercial contract</u>

It will depend on the type of agreement as to which clauses are important (for example, the banking team will be looking at events of default in the loan documentation).

The best approach would be for each area of practice (e.g., the corporate team/employment team/banking team etc.) to have a separate checklist for each type of document. A good team briefing prior to undertaking the due diligence exercise would ascertain the key issues for each department and aids this checklist preparation.

Client's concerns

The content of your teams checklist will also depend on what your client's key concerns are – for example, if the acquisition is taking place because they wish to acquire a particular contract (and they propose to terminate the remainder of the contracts after completion), you will be focussing on termination clauses (and consequences of termination) for the majority of the contracts and analysing the particular contract that they are interested in, in more depth.

Parties

This goes back to the advice raised in Chapter 1 - to use your diagram of the transaction and the parties whenever you are working on the transaction.

When you are reviewing a key contract, the first item to check must always be the parties – are the parties who have entered the contract, the parties to whom the agreement relates?

A common issue for example is when looking at intellectual property licences, the parties to the licence are often not the actual users of the intellectual property in practice. This is a particularly common issue when you have lots of companies in a group – therefore always take care to be clear on who the parties to each contract are (and ascertain if they are in fact the correct parties).

Date of the agreement/term/termination

Check the date the agreement commenced and how long the agreement was for. You are checking this to ensure the agreement has actually started (for example, was it subject to conditions precedent that have not been satisfied or was it left in draft and negotiations were not completed – see execution below) and once it has begun, is it due to terminate shortly? If the agreement is a key contract, it is a significant issue if it is due to expire in the near future and no action has been taken to renew etc. It may be as simple as asking for more information to ascertain whereabouts in the renewal process the parties are up to.

It is also important to ascertain what happens on termination (for example are fees due/compensation/written notice required) and what would permit either party to the contract to terminate (i.e., can you terminate with notice if your clients' intentions are to terminate post completion or does the contract only permit termination for breach (and what actions constitute a breach).

Execution

Linked closely to the date and term of the agreement is execution – you must check to ensure that each agreement has been properly executed – have you been given the signature pages for both parties? It is common in practice that contracts are drafted and then not entered into. Again, this would be a key issue if this is an important contract.

As well as ensuring the relevant agreement has been signed by all parties, it is also important to check who the signatories were – as you need to check whether the parties who signed the contract had the proper authority to enter into the agreement. For example, if the third party is a company, check to see if there were named directors signing on behalf of the third party (so you will need to do a Companies House search on the third party) and ask to see a board minute from the third party authorising those individuals to sign that contract.

> Practical tip: Make sure you have all of the pages of the contract, that they are legible (i.e., have they been scanned properly and are readable) and that it has been signed and dated by the correct parties.

Change of control/prohibition on assignment

As noted above, we are looking to see if any third-party consent is needed here.

Other issues

There will be other issues depending on the type of the contract, including without limitation:

- Is the agreement effective (for example was proper consideration provided by both parties or was it signed as a deed or is it too vague/does it contain agreements to agree and is unenforceable)?
- Is the Target under confidentiality obligations under this contract/has there been any breach?
- Retention of title? Does the third party have any retention of title over the subject of the contract?
- Have warranties been given by the Target? What is the scope of these warranties?
- Have any separate indemnities or guarantees been provided? The extent of each of these should be noted as can lead to future liability for the Target. Likewise, if the third party or Target has their liability limited or excluded, the extent of the limitations should be noted.
- Restrictive covenants? Has the third party or Target been restricted in their future behaviour (and if so, are these restrictions likely to be

enforceable)? See Chapter 9 for the additional considerations in relation to the enforceability of restrictive covenants).

- What law governs the contract? If the law is outside the UK, you may need external advice as to the implications of the contract.
- Are there any other unusual terms that should be noted?

Examples of key issues to look for in the corporate data

See the analysis in the corporate information section below.

Practical tip: Ensure you are comfortable with what you need to do before starting your due diligence review, including understanding:

- the scope of due diligence to be carried out (i.e., are you clear on the level of due diligence you are delving into)/check the written scope agreed with the client;
- the items of key importance to the client – add these to your checklists; and
- how to communicate a deal breaker/urgent issue you discover.

Helpful hints:

- If you are unsure as to how to start, ask to review the data room index with your supervisor before you begin looking at documents to flag up areas to focus your attention.
- Prepare and use a checklist for reviewing all key documents (and ensure all the team members conducting the due diligence use the same checklist where appropriate) – it will assist you with your consistency in reporting.

Questionnaires

The due diligence process is usually started by a questionnaire being sent from the buyer to the Seller(s). Normally, most corporate teams have a standard share sale and a standard business sale questionnaire that they use. However, the more that the questionnaire is tailored to the transaction, the better the responses will be. Take your time to read the questionnaire carefully thinking about the information that you already have about the transaction and tailor it to fit the transaction as much as possible.

Other sources of information

The buyer's team should not solely rely on the information provided by the Seller(s) but should also use other information in the public domain to verify the Seller's information and provide a full picture to the buyer. Some suggestions to the types of information in the public domain and what you are looking for are set out below.

Corporate information - overview

This can include searches at Companies House but who you search against will depend on the type of the transaction (see below).

These searches should be carried out at the beginning of the due diligence process and then again just before exchange/completion of the transaction to ensure nothing has changed since the date of the original searches.

If you are advising on a share sale, the buyer should always do a search on the Target and any subsidiaries of the Target together with any companies the Target holds shares in, the Seller (if it is a company) and any companies that may be acting as guarantors in the transaction. Chapter 9 illustrates when guarantors are more likely to be utilised.

If the sale is a business sale, the search will need to be against the corporate seller (this goes back to what we looked at in Chapter 3 – the trading company is now the Seller) and any corporate parents and guarantors.

When undertaking a company search – the first thing to do is look at the filing history which shows you all the items the company has filed at Companies House. The overview page will show you when the CS01 (confirmation statement) and accounts are/were due and if any filings are late. If some items are not filed, there may be a default fine, but this does not protect the buyer so would need to be dealt with as part of the transactional documentation. It may also underline that there are other issues taking place (as a key question would be why the accounts or confirmation statement may be late).

Key documents to check as part of the search are the annual accounts, CS01 (which replaced the Annual Return), details of all of the directors and secretary (if applicable) and the People Having Significant Control (which is included on a separate tab of the search), memorandum of association, latest set of articles of association (see below) and any security (charges) over the company's assets. You would also look to see if there are any liquidation or winding up resolutions, new share allotments and any recent special or ordinary resolutions (which are resolutions of the shareholders).

Check that all the information in the public domain matches the structure chart you have compiled based on the information provided by the Seller(s). Remember it goes back to the fundamental issue that you need to ensure the buyer acquires good title to the shares on a share sale (which means you must be completely comfortable and confident as to who the owner of the shares is).

In addition to the search at Companies House, you would also look at additional corporate information to ensure no winding up petitions have been lodged. You should start by searching for details of companies involved in insolvency proceedings on The Gazette's website. You can then check to see if the Target is being liquidated (and whether the company is in provisional liquidation which would mean the Target's assets have been frozen in advance of a hearing to decide if it should be liquidated via the Insolvency Service website (PIU Database Results (bis.gov.uk)).

In addition, you should review the Companies House disqualified directors register which includes details of directors disqualified by the courts and the Insolvency Service (e.g., you should not be negotiating with a disqualified director unless they have had the courts permission to continue as a director).

Other searches

Other searches to be undertaken will depend on the nature of the transaction, such as an FCA search (https://register.fca.org.uk) (which lists all firms and individuals involved in regulated activities so you can check what they are regulated to do and their permissions and activities), the intellectual property office (to search separately for each of patents, registered trademarks and registered design information), property searches (e.g. including the Local Land Charges Registry, Land Registry and Land Charges).

In addition, a news search should be conducted together with a general online search relating to the Target and its directors and shareholders.

Web addresses for the separate intellectual property searches are as follows:

- Trademark search: https://www.gov.uk/topic/intellectual-property/trade-marks
- Patent search: https://www.gov.uk/topic/intellectual-property/patents
- Registered design search: https://www.gov.uk/search-registered-design

Statutory registers

You would ask to see the statutory registers (which are usually located at the registered office or a Single Alternative Inspection Location ("**SAIL**")).

The Small Business, Enterprise and Employment Act 2015 allowed a private company from 30 June 2016 to choose to send information usually retained in their statutory registers to be kept on the public register at Companies House. This is an alternative to retaining the registers at its registered office or the SAIL, and you will be able to ascertain this from the Companies House search. If they have elected to retain their registers at Companies House, the company is still required to maintain its historic registers up to the date they elected to retain them at Companies House (and these should be handed over in the same way (see below)).The majority of private companies have not elected to keep their registers at Companies House and instead will retain them at the registered office/SAIL as noted above.

The Target will be required to hand over the statutory registers on completion of a share sale, so they need to be inspected in advance to ensure they are accurate, up to date and reflect the buyer's understanding of the structure of the Target.

Your aim when analysing both the statutory registers (and all of the information provided) is that the Seller(s) owns what they say they own (for example, it is vital to ensure if some shares have been bought back from previous shareholders, to ensure the out-going shareholder was removed from the register of members). You must also ascertain whether there has been additional security lodged over the shares (which would prevent the shares from being freely transferred).

You must compare the information in the statutory registers to the information you have ascertained from your own searches at Companies House (to ensure the information tallies – if not, there is either an error in the registers or in the external filings that will need addressing prior to completion of the transaction).

The statutory registers constitute of:

- Register of members

  The register of members is a fundamental document required to be kept under s.113 Companies Act 2006 ("**CA 2006**") and it tells us who the legal owner of the shares is – if there are errors that go beyond typographical errors, a court application for rectification of the register will be required prior to completion pursuant to s.125 CA 2006.

  This goes back to the fundamental reason for due diligence – you are ascertaining whether the Seller(s) own the shares on a share sale and whether they are free to sell to the buyer and that the buyer will acquire good title to the shares. For example, the register may reveal that there are minority shareholders that have not been party to the negotiations. If these minority shareholdings are not acquired as part of the acquisition, this could cause issues for the buyer after completion (as they will not own 100% of the Target and will not be able to act freely).

- Register of directors (and separate register of directors' residential addresses)

- Register of secretaries (if applicable)

- Register of debentures

- People Having Significant Control Register

- Register of charges

  The law in relation to the register of charges changed in 2013. There is no requirement to keep a register of charges for any charges created on or after 6 April 2013, however it is required for any charges prior to that date (therefore there may be a historic register in relation to charges that predate the change in law) (and charges must still be registered at Companies House within 21 days of creation of the charge otherwise they are void against the liquidator or administrator).

  As noted in Chapter 3, it is fundamental to be clear on the form of your sale. On a share sale, it is vital to check no charges have been created over the shares in the Target (and that the Target has not created any charges over its assets). On an asset sale, you must ascertain whether there are any charges over any of the assets that form part of the sale.

Any charges in place will need to be dealt with as part of the completion process (e.g., they will either need to be released or certificates of non-crystallisation will be required).

Memorandum of association

Your Companies House search will tell you when the company was incorporated – if it was incorporated before 1 October 2009, it will have been incorporated prior to the CA 2006. This will mean it will have a different memorandum of association to a company incorporated under the CA 2006.

This old-style memorandum will need reviewing (if it has not been superseded by later filings by the Target) as the CA 2006 under s.28 CA 2006 deems anything in the old-style memorandum is treated as being part of the articles of association. An old-style memorandum would potentially have included a number of items that require checking:

- Objects clause
- Authorised share capital
- Liability of the company

A company incorporated under CA 2006 has a standard form memorandum (which no longer forms part of the constitution).

Some companies who retained old-style memorandum have amended their articles (which has then effectively removed the significance of the old memorandum). If they have made this change, you will need to check what has been included in the new articles (e.g., have they no longer got an objects clause) and that the statement of liability has been included in the articles.

Articles of association

This is an important document to review as part of the due diligence process.

The articles of association are often referred to as the constitution of the company. They are a statutory contract between the company, the members (this is the shareholders in a private company limited by shares) and the members themselves under s33 CA 2006. As well as being a contract that binds these shareholders, the directors of the Target have a duty to act in accordance with the constitution.

The articles of association may contain sections that impact on the process of the transaction, such as pre-emption rights on share transfers, which mean that the Seller(s) have to offer their shares to any other existing shareholders instead of the prospective buyer (and these rights would therefore need to be waived as part of the completion process), requirements for shareholder approval or limits on what the board of directors can do. They will also set out the practicalities required for any meetings required by the Target's board of directors, or any resolutions required by the Target's shareholders as part of the transaction process (such as notice of the meetings and the number of directors/shareholders required to attend for a valid board or shareholder meeting).

In addition to considering what needs to be carried out to achieve completion of the transaction, the articles of association together with all applicable filings/resolutions and minutes would also need to be checked to ensure that any changes to share capital (such as allotments, transfers, subdivision, consolidation etc. prior to the transaction were carried out properly with the appropriate authorisations. As noted above, this is particularly important if any shares were bought back from shareholders previously by the Target or if any changes to the share capital have been made.

In practice, if the Target has carried out a buyback of own shares (for example, from a shareholder who was an employee who resigned or was dismissed), if the buyback had not been conducted properly, there would be a risk that the (potentially disgruntled) ex-employee may still retain shares in the Target, which could have serious consequences for a proposed sale (as the Seller will not own 100% of the shares and the ex-employee may not wish to co-operate in sale).

These issues are outside the scope of this text but illustrate the key issue of ensuring the Seller(s) own title to the shares (and no other person has any interest/ownership in or over the shares being sold).

Board minutes

In an ideal world, the company will have board minutes of any decisions taken outside the ordinary course of business as well as having board minutes of any regular board meeting.

Board minutes are useful source of information, and you would expect to see minutes relating to acquisitions, declaration of dividends, buyback of shares, borrowing, litigation, taking security etc. They assist in illustrating whether proper processes have been followed.

A review of minutes provided may highlight other documentation that has not been provided (e.g., loans etc.) which would need to be reviewed as part of the due diligence process.

Employee issues

In addition to the corporate and commercial due diligence issues noted above, there are a number of key employee issues to consider as part of the due diligence review.

Contractual entitlements following changes in ownership

A buyer needs to be mindful of entitlements that an employee may have which are then triggered by the sale. For example, there could have been some negotiation regarding sale bonuses or a "golden parachute". Clearly the impact of these will need to be taken into consideration when negotiating the purchase price, as well as considering whether or not contracts of employment can be changed post completion. The buyer may well want to seek a reduction in price or ensure that the cost of these additional employee entitlements are borne by the Seller(s). The transferee also needs to consider additional rights on change of control, for example enhanced termination compensation and contractual redundancy schemes

Contractual benefits that are not transferred

There are some contractual benefits, by their very nature which cannot be transferred, for example share options and profit share schemes may cause some issues.

Lawyers will need to ask what the buyer intends to do about such schemes and best advice would be that the transferee should provide a similar scheme replicating the scheme that has been lost as far as possible. If not, it may be necessary to change employee's terms and conditions although, clearly practitioners need to be mindful of the significant protection that TUPE offers employees in the circumstances and the difficulties associated with harmonisation.

Hidden employees

Careful consideration to the due diligence responses is vital to identify any employees who are not expressly stated to be transferring to the buyer on the sale of the business. Close inspection of the circumstances may be that employees are in fact assigned to the undertaking being sold - that is a question of fact, and as such they are then automatically transferred to the buyer even if they have not been identified. Therefore, the buyer may wish to seek an indemnity in respect of any hidden employees.

Restrictive covenants

As we have seen in a business sale, restrictive covenants will transfer to a transferee on a TUPE transfer. The transferee will need to consider whether the restrictions are still enforceable after a transfer when the identity of the employer has clearly changed. See ***Morris Angel & Son Limited v Hollande [1993] IRLR 169.***

From a practical perspective, transferees should consider entering into new restrictive covenants with key transferring employees, ensuring customers who dealt with the employee both prior to and following the transfer are protected. Transferees should also be aware of the risks of changing those terms and conditions post transfer.

Immigration

If an employee does not have the right to work, and therefore is employed illegally and without permission to work in the UK, employers could be fined up to £20,000 for each illegal worker, unless they have carried out specific checks on an individual before employing them to ensure they are eligible to work in the UK.

Following a TUPE transfer the UK Border Agency expect the transferee to carry out its own checks within 60 days, regardless of whether comprehensive checks were carried out by the transferor prior to the transfer.

Legal claims

Clearly the cost of litigation is an important factor, and the parties need to consider any potential claims that may arise and balance that risk. Close attention needs to be paid to the due diligence exercise so that risks can be clearly identified and managed.

<u>Data rooms</u>

The Seller(s) will respond to the questionnaire with answers and supporting documentation, which will be placed in the "data room" (see below for what this means). The Seller will need to carefully consider what documentation a prospective buyer will need to see whilst protecting commercially sensitive information as much as possible (see staggered due diligence suggestion below). If insufficient information is provided, the Buyer is likely to raise additional due diligence enquiries.

A data room may take one of two forms – it may either be a live data room or, more likely, it will be a virtual data room.

Whichever form the data room takes, the Buyer's advisers will be required to sign up to data room rules and the Seller(s) team should ensure the documents are grouped sensibly and a clear index is provided (and updated every time additional documentation is added to the data room).

Live data room

A live data room is simply a physical room where the due diligence documents are kept for inspection by the buyer. They are usually at the Seller's solicitor's offices, and the buyer's advisers will travel to attend the data room and will review the documents at the times agreed between the parties. Live data rooms are usually supervised by a member of the deal team (for example one of the trainee solicitors involved in the transaction).

Virtual data room

Even prior to the Covid-19 pandemic, the more common form of data rom is now a virtual data room. This is an internet-based portal/room where the due diligence documents are uploaded. It means that they can be accessed from any location (and can be accessed simultaneously by the advisors) and can be accessed at any time (so the due diligence can be conducted 24/7).

A virtual data room provider should be utilised (and many larger firms have their own portal/software that can be used). It should be noted that a virtual data room is not simply sharing documents via cloud storage (and sites such as Dropbox or Google Docs are not appropriate tools for this process).

There may be restrictions set on whether the documents in the virtual data room can be downloaded/printed and access to the documents can also be restricted e.g., only permitting the employment solicitors to review the employment documentation. It should be noted that even if the documents are "locked", an unscrupulous buyer can still elect to breach the data room rules and circumvent these protections by taking photographs of the protected documents. The only way to avoid this is to have a supervised data room (which is usually the most common reason for utilising a live data room – where a document is so sensitive that the Seller(s) cannot risk it being copied).

The Seller(s) can often use the diagnostic tools provided by the virtual data room to see how much time the Buyer and their team have spent undertaking the due diligence and even the length of time individuals within the team have spent looking at particular documents, which can assist in the negotiation process (as the Seller will have an idea of the buyer concerns in advance and can prepare to deal with any particular issues). It can also provide liability protection for the Seller(s) in the future as they can identify that a buyer has seen a particular document.

Data protection

The data protection issues in relation to placing information in the data room are outside the scope of this text. However, the aim would be to ensure all personal data from all documentation placed in the data room is redacted so no personal information is provided as part of the due diligence process (e.g., redacting names, addresses, email addresses, job titles etc prior to putting the data within the data room).

Types of information included in the data room

The types of information included in the data room will vary on each transaction and the Seller(s) will also need to consider in advance how they wish to deal with commercially sensitive documentation such as redacting sensitive parts of key contracts, providing reports summarising contractual arrangements or staggering some of the documentation by retaining the commercially sensitive documentation until a second phase of due diligence (to ensure the buyer is sufficiently engaged in the negotiation process etc.). There are also additional issues if there are any litigation matters to be disclosed and you will need to take advice from the litigation team on how to protect legal professional privilege.

> Practical tip: If you are acting for the buyer, be clear on how you will be alerted to any additions to the data room – as a corporate support lawyer/member of the employment team reviewing the employment documents, you do not want to think you have reviewed all of the employment contracts and prepared your section of the due diligence report, only to find that another raft of employee documents were added to the data room a week later.

Reporting

Once you have reviewed all of the relevant information, the buyer's advisors will need to report on the things that have been discovered.

It is always important to consider your audience – are you writing for the Chief Executive Officer or the board of directors? Are they laymen? Are they experienced professionals who have been through previous acquisitions and will be familiar with legal terms and their implications, or is this the only transaction they have been involved in and they are overwhelmed with the issues and the legal terms utilised?

Once you have considered the way in which you will pitch your report, you then need to draft your report in the form agreed as part of the scope of due diligence. Reports can take a number of forms:

- interim;
- long form; or
- exceptions only.

Regardless of the form, it is always recommended to include an executive summary at the beginning of your report, ensuring you draw the key issues to the client's attention at the outset (based around the assumption that the client may not review the due diligence report in its entirety), so you are drawing fundamental points to their attention.

As well as raising the issues that you have discovered, your report should also include suggestions of how to deal with these concerns/consider contractual protections for the buyer to consider, such as requesting further information, negotiating an adjustment in price, seeking third party consent, requesting further warranties and/or indemnities or in the event of a serious issue, considering whether to walk away from the transaction or considering a restructuring from a share sale to the sale of the business as a going concern).

The report should also be divided into sensible sections (usually looking at each area of the Target), e.g., corporate, accounting, commercial, employment, pensions etc.

Interim

Interim reports are usually only for lengthy and large transactions – they are used to draw the buyer's attention to any key issues that need to be appreciated as part of the negotiation process. It would include flagging any serious/deal breaker issues that the client must be immediately told about.

Long form

This is the most expensive form of report to prepare for the client as it includes a complete review of the Target, or the business being purchased. This would include a detailed summary of the terms of each of the contracts that the Target is party to (and provides a useful illustration of when a checklist is hugely helpful – if a checklist has been used when reviewing each of the contracts, it is very easy to put this completed checklist into a schedule to the due diligence report).

Exceptions only

This is the most common form of report – which only includes issues that are material to the transaction (including any unusual issues or any issues that can result in liability or reduction in value of the Target or the business). There is also usually a summary of the corporate structure in addition to the issues discovered.

> Practical tip: Be clear what form of reporting you are required to use (exceptions only or long form) and ideally, ask for a precedent/ template report (to ensure all of the members of the deal team are all using the same terms throughout).

CHAPTER SIX

THE EMPLOYMENT ISSUES IN MERGERS AND ACQUISITIONS

Introduction

We have explored in Chapter 3 there are two ways of purchasing a business – the purchase of a business or a share purchase. Now that you appreciate the difference, we are now going to consider the implications for employment law under Transfer of Undertakings (Protection of Employment) Regulations 2006 ("**TUPE**") in a corporate transaction.

As a reminder - in a share sale, the only item that is sold are the shares in the Target. As nothing else changes, the only thing that is being altered is the ownership of the business which is being transferred from the Seller(s) to the buyer after completion. To the outside world, the business remains exactly the same before and after completion. Therefore, it has been a long-established principle that TUPE does not apply to share sales. This is because in order for TUPE to be triggered there needs to be a change in the identity of the employer, and where shares are transferred it is only the legal identity of the shareholders of the Target that changes, not the identity of the employer.

As noted in Chapter 3, where there is the sale of the business, the business is sold as a going concern. This means that a buyer is agreeing to purchase individual assets that make up the business (e.g., plant, machinery, goodwill etc.). In asset sales there are significant implications for employees under TUPE. This is because the regulations will apply where there is an asset transfer.

So, in this chapter we are going to explore TUPE and the implications of the regulations where there is a transfer of the assets. TUPE will apply when there is a "**Relevant Transfer**", so let's ask ourselves the following questions:

What is a relevant transfer?

TUPE applies to a relevant transfer. This definition covers two scenarios:

- A transfer of a business, undertaking or part of a business or undertaking where there is a transfer of an economic entity that retains its identity (a "business transfer") (R*egulation 3(1)(a), TUPE).*
- A client engaging a contractor to do work on its behalf, reassigning such a contract or bringing the work back in house (a "service provision change") (R*egulation 3(1)(b), TUPE).*

Business transfers

The first part of the definition of a relevant transfer is set out in *Regulation 3(1)(a), TUPE:*

> "A transfer of an undertaking, business or part of an undertaking or business situated immediately before the transfer in the United Kingdom to another person where there is a transfer of an economic entity which retains its identity."

There are three elements to this:

- There must be an economic entity;
- There must be a transfer of that economic entity; and
- The economic entity must retain its identity following the transfer.

Is there an identifiable economic entity?

TUPE defines an "economic entity" as "an organised grouping of resources that has the objective of pursuing an economic activity, whether or not that activity is central or ancillary" (*Regulation 3(2)*). This follows the test set out by the ECJ in ***Süzen v Gebaüdereinigung GmbH [1997] IRLR 255*** in which an economic entity was defined as "an organised grouping of persons and assets facilitating the exercise of an economic activity which pursues a specific objective".

Sometimes it is clear when something amounts to an economic entity. For example, the sale of the all the assets of a company to a single buyer will amount to the sale and transfer of an economic entity.

However, if the assets are being sold or transferred to different buyers, it is necessary to determine whether each separate sale or transfer is the sale or transfer of an identifiable economic entity. See also ***Balfour Beatty Power Networks Ltd v Wilcox [2007] IRLR 63.***

The transfer of part of an undertaking or business – is this an economic entity?

TUPE can apply to the transfer of all or part of an undertaking or business. Case law has established that the relevant part must be a self-contained and be a potentially severable economic unit. Further, the assets making up that part must be sufficiently grouped to constitute an economic entity in their own right, that is, they should be assigned to the performance of the objectives of that economic entity see ***Fairhurst Ward Abbotts v Botes Building Ltd [2004] IRLR 304.***

Is there a transfer of the economic entity?

TUPE applies to a transfer "howsoever effected" (R*egulation 3(4)(b) and by Regulation 3(6). This includes a* transfer by one or a series of transactions (whether or not between the same parties) *see* ***Foreningen af Arbejdsledere i Danmark v Daddy's Dance Hall [1988] IRLR 315) ECJ.***

Does the economic entity retain its identity?
Let's explore the useful decision of ***Spijkers v Gebroeders Benedik Abattoir CV*: 24/85** *[1986]* ***2CMLR 296 ECJ*** which lays down the basic definition of a transfer of an undertaking retaining its identity.

In ***Spijkers*** the ECJ held that:

> *"it is necessary to determine whether what has been sold is an economic entity which is still in existence, and this will be apparent from the fact that the operation is actually being continued or has been taken over by the new employer within the same economic or similar activity."*

In order to decide whether there is a transfer the ECJ stated that following matters should be considered:

a) the type of undertaking involved;
b) whether there was a transfer of assets;
c) the value of intangible assets such as goodwill;
d) whether and how many staff are taken on;

e) transfer of customers;
f) similarity of activities before and after the transfer;
g) the duration of any interruption of services.

The importance of any of the factors will vary considerably according to the nature of the transaction.

Is there a service provision change?

It has long been established that TUPE can apply to a change of contractor. TUPE now expressly states that there is a relevant transfer where there is a service provision change.

Regulation 3(1)(b) of TUPE 2006 defines a service provision change as a situation in which:

"(i) activities cease to be carried out by a person ("a client") on his own behalf and are carried out instead by another person on the client's behalf ("a contractor");

(ii) activities cease to be carried out by a contractor on a client's behalf (whether or not those activities had previously been carried out by the client on his own behalf) and are carried out instead by another person ("a subsequent contractor") on the client's behalf; or

(iii) activities cease to be carried out by a contractor or a subsequent contractor on a client's behalf (whether or not those activities had previously been carried out by the client on his own behalf) and are carried out instead by the client on his own behalf, and in which the conditions set out in paragraph (3) are satisfied."

Note that "contractor" also means sub-contractor (*Regulation 2(1), TUPE*).

In order for there to be a service provision change covered by TUPE the following must be present:

- An organised grouping of employees situated in Great Britain before the change whose principal purpose is carrying on services for the client (*Regulation 3(3)(a)(i), TUPE*).
- The organised grouping of employees could be a single employee (*Regulation 2(1), TUPE*).

- The organised grouping must have, as its principal purpose, the provision of services to a particular client.

As we have considered, for there to be a business transfer, there must be a transfer of an economic entity which retains its identity, which will involve the transfer of some assets (see above). Where there is a service provision the transfer of assets will not happen, it is merely necessary for one person to cease to provide the activities and for another to take them over

The term "principal purpose" means that the employees must be "essentially dedicated" to the relevant activity see ***Eddie Stobart Ltd v Moreman and others UKEAT 0223/11***

Practical tip: as a practitioner ensure you appreciate the difference between an asset sale and a service provision change under TUPE.

What is the effect of TUPE on the employee's contracts of employment?

Where there is a relevant transfer for the purposes of Regulation 3 of TUPE the transfer does not terminate the employment contracts of the employees affected. Instead, the employment contracts of employees employed by the transferor and assigned to the organised grouping of resources or employees that is subject to the relevant transfer have effect after the transfer as if originally made between such employees and the transferee. (*Regulation 4(1), TUPE*).

Who transfers?

Employees

Under TUPE, only employees employed by the transferor immediately before the transfer will transfer to the new employer.

Regulation 4(3) TUPE provides that the automatic transfer principle applies to anyone employed in the organised grouping of resources or employees "immediately before" the transfer or who would have been so employed if they had not been dismissed because of the transfer or a reason connected with it which is not an ETO reason entailing changes in the numbers of the workforce. This ensures that employees who are dismissed by the transferor before the transfer will have a right of action against the transferee as liability for their dismissals will automatically transfer to them under TUPE. If however the pre transfer dismissal is entirely unconnected to the transfer or connected to the transfer but for an ETO reason employees will not be deemed to be employed immediately before the transfer. In this scenario, liability for their dismissals will therefore remain with the transferor.

> Practical tips:
>
> Ensure:
>
> - you carefully identify who was assigned to work in the business being transferred;
> - indemnities cover any claims by employees who should have been on the list but were not, and conversely, giving assurance to the transferor that the transferee has not taken the opportunity of the transfer to 'dump' employees it did not want into the transferring business.

The right to object

Employees have the right to object to their transfer to a new employer under TUPE by informing either the transferor or the transferee of their objection (*Regulation 4(7) TUPE*). However, if they do, their employment with the transferor is deemed to terminate by operation of law with effect from the transfer date. Since there is no dismissal or resignation in these circumstances, employees who object to the transfer are not entitled to any statutory or contractual compensation on termination (see ***Marcroft v Heartland (Midlands) Limited [2011] EWCA Civ 438).***

What transfers under TUPE?

On a TUPE transfer, all of the transferor's rights, powers, duties and liabilities under or in connection with the transferring employees' contracts pass to the buyer (*Regulation 4(2)(a) TUPE*). The major exception is pension rights because they are expressly excluded by Regulation 10(1) of TUPE.

Any acts or omissions of the transferor done or not done before the transfer are treated as having been done by the transferee (*Regulation 4(2)(b) TUPE*).

The automatic transfer principle extends to all rights and benefits (such as holiday pay, medical and permanent health insurance, collective agreements, any trade union recognition, company car schemes, bonus or commission schemes, profit share schemes, maternity schemes and redundancy schemes), both contractual and statutory (see ***Jackson v Computershare Investor Services PLC [2007] CA Civ 1065***).

Information and consultation obligations

Prior to a TUPE transfer there is an obligation on both the transferor and transferee to inform and consult with a recognised trade union or elected employee representatives.

What is the duty to inform?

The obligation to provide information falls upon both the transferor and transferee. Regulation 13(2) TUPE sets out what information must be disclosed by employers to the appropriate representatives to enable consultations to take place.

The information that is required must include:

- the fact that the transfer is to take place;
- approximately when it is to take place;
- the reason for the transfer;
- the legal, economic and social implications of the transfer for affected employees (this definition has no interpretative assistance and is a straight lift from the directive itself);
- the measures that the employer envisages it will take in relation to affected employees in connection with the transfer;
- where employees are to be transferred –
- the transferee must decide whether he intends to take measures in

relation to any employees and he must tell the transferor that he does not envisage changes or detail the changes that are envisaged;

- the transferor must pass on this information to the unions in respect of those employees.

Who must be informed?

Regulation 13(1) TUPE states that "affected employees" means not only employees who are to be transferred to a new employer but any other employee of the transferor or of the transferee who may be affected by the transfer or who may be affected by 'measures taken' in connection with the transfer.

What is meant by "measures taken" is not defined but can encompass any significant alteration in existing working practices. The duty is therefore to provide information not only to employees who transfer but also to those will not transfer but who will be affected by the transfer taking effect.

The transferee will also be under an obligation to provide information to its own employees who will be affected by the transfer of new employees into its business. In some circumstances employers may be under a duty to consult with all of its employees about a transfer.

> Practical tip: The term "affected employee" is restricted to employees of the relevant employer. Employees of associated employers are not affected employees.

When does the employer have to inform and consult?

Under Regulation 13(2) TUPE the duty on the employer is to provide information long enough before the transfer to enable consultation to take place. Regulation 13(2)(a) states that appropriate representatives must be given information about the "fact that the relevant transfer is to take place".

Employee representatives are entitled to be consulted by the employer "as soon as reasonably practicable after the election of the representatives".

See Banking Insurance and Finance Union v Barclays Bank PLC [1987] ICR 495 and Amicus v UCATT [2009] EAT.

The duty to consult

The duty to provide information applies to every transfer but the duty to consult only arises where the relevant employer envisages that he will be taking measures in relation to any affected employee and the duty is to consult the appropriate representatives in respect of that category of employee. Under Regulation 13(6) TUPE the duty to consult should be taken with a view to "seeking agreement to measures to be taken".

The transferor is obliged to consult with the appropriate representatives of its own employees in relation to whom it envisages that it will be taking measures either before or after the transfer. The transferor does not have to consult with representatives of employees who will transfer, as it will be the transferee who will be proposing to take measures in relation to them after the transfer. The only duty in relation to the transferring of employees is to provide the appropriate representatives with information concerning measures the transferee will envisage that it will take.

The transferee is under a duty to consult with the appropriate representatives of the transferring employees once the transfer has taken place. Regulation 13 TUPE does not require them to consult with such representatives prior to the transfer taking place.

The purpose of consultation must be undertaken "with a view to seeking the appropriate representatives' agreement of the measures to be taken". This does not mean that agreement must be reached. Under Regulation 13(7) TUPE the employer must consider representations made by appropriate representatives and reply to those representations. If the employer rejects those representations, it must state the reason for doing so.

The appropriate representatives

Employers are obliged to inform and consult with appropriate representatives of their own employees who may be affected by the transfer or measures that will be taken in connection with such transfer. "Appropriate Representative" is defined in Regulation 13(3) TUPE. Appropriate Representatives are representatives of an independent trade union, which is recognised by the employer.

Where affected employees are not members of a recognised union the employer can choose to consult with the following:

- employees who have been appointed or elected otherwise than for specific purposes of TUPE by the affected employees but who, given the purpose and mode of their appointment or election, have the authority from affected employees to receive information and to be consulted on their behalf (i.e., Information and consultation reps under the 2002 Regulations); or

- Employees elected by the affected employees for the specific purpose of being given information or being consulted by the employer under TUPE in an election satisfying Regulation 14.

Employers therefore do not have an option of choosing whether or not to consult with a recognised Trade Union.

The election of appropriate representatives

The election procedure is set out in Regulation 14 TUPE. If the employees fail to elect representatives within a reasonable time, the employer must give to each affected employee the information that they would otherwise give to the appropriate representatives.

All appropriate representatives are given protection under TUPE including:

- access to all affected employees;
- access to such accommodation and facilities as may be appropriate (*Regulation 13(8)*);
- the right to claim automatic unfair dismissal and victimisation arising out of dismissals or any detriment suffered as a consequence of acting as an appropriate representative or taking part in an election for an appropriate representative; and
- the right to time off work with pay in order to train for and undertake duties as an appropriate representative.

Businesses with fewer than 10 employees

Under regulation 13A of TUPE, employers with fewer than 10 employees may discharge their obligations to inform and consult appropriate representatives by informing and consulting affected employees directly where there are no existing appropriate representatives.

Transferee may consult with transferor's employees in certain circumstances

The Collective Redundancies and Transfer of Undertakings (Protection of Employment)(Amendment) Regulations 2014 added new S.198A and S.198B to the Trade Union and Labour Relations (Consolidation) Act 1992 with effect from 31 January 2014.

Under these provisions, where the transferee is proposing to make collective redundancies and one or more of the transferring employees may be affected, the transferee may, if certain conditions are satisfied, elect to commence consultation with representatives of the transferring employees while they are still employed by the transferor.

Defences for failure to inform or consult

An employer has a defence for failure to inform or consult if it can show that there were special circumstances making it not reasonably practicable for information to be given or consultation to take place, and that it had done the best it could to comply in the circumstances (*Regulation 13(9) TUPE*).

However, in practice, this defence is construed very narrowly. The fact of commercial confidentiality is not necessarily regarded as being sufficient reason to make the defence available. While a Tribunal may appreciate that it is necessary for a deal to be kept confidential up to the moment when contracts are exchanged, the general view is that there is nothing stopping a seller and buyer from providing a reasonable period of time between exchange and completion to allow the information and consultation processes to run their course.

<u>Remedies available to appropriate representatives and employees</u>

Where an employer fails to comply with the duty to inform and consult, the appropriate representatives can make a complaint to the Employment Tribunal. Complaints can be made to the Tribunal on the following grounds (*Regulation 14 TUPE*):

- complaints regarding the election of appropriate representatives by any affected employee;
- complaints relating to appropriate representatives may be made by the representatives to whom the failure relates;
- complaints relating to trade union representatives may be made by the Trade Union concerned; and
- any other complaints may be made by the affected employees.

Liability for claims

Where a Tribunal finds a complaint well-founded, it will make a declaration to that effect and may award compensation payable to the relevant affected employees of up to **13 weeks' gross pay** for each affected employee. There is no limit on the amount of a week's pay.

If the Tribunal upholds a claim against the transferee, it may order the transferee to pay appropriate compensation to the affected employees (*Regulation 15(7) TUPE*).

If the Tribunal upholds a claim against the transferor, it may order the transferor to pay appropriate compensation to the affected employees or, where the transferor establishes that it failed to inform or consult because the transferee had not given it the relevant information, order the transferee to pay the compensation (R*egulation 15(8, TUPE*). In these cases, the transferor must notify the transferee that it intends to rely on the transferor's non-compliance with Regulation 13(4) for its failure to comply with its consultation obligations, and the transferee becomes a party to the proceedings (*Regulation 15(5) TUPE*).

Joint and several liability

In circumstances where the transferor has breached its obligations to inform and consult, under Regulation 15(9) TUPE the Tribunal can make the transferee and the transferor jointly and severally liable for:

- any compensation awarded by the Tribunal against the transferor for failure to inform and consult;

- any failure by the transferor or the transferee to pay compensation that has been ordered by the Tribunal for a failure to inform or consult.

Employee liability information – Regulation 11 and 12

These provisions oblige all transferors to provide employee liability information to the transferee and this includes information of any employee who is to transfer. This information must be in writing. Note that the information has to be provided to transferees, not prospective transferees.

Changes to terms of employment

Regulation 4(4) states that contractual changes would only be void if the sole or principal reason for the change is either the transfer itself or a reason connected with a transfer which is not an economic, technical or organisational reason entailing changes in the workforce ("**ETO**").

Changes to terms of employment are permitted for an ETO reason where the employer and employee both agree to the change or if the terms of the contract permit the employer to make the variation. See Collective Redundancies and Transfer of Undertakings (Protection of Employment) (Amendment) Regulations 2014 SI 2014/16.

There will only be an ETO if there is a change in the numbers or possibly functions of the workforce (see ***Delabole Slate Co Ltd v Berriman [1985] IRLR 305)***.

Practical tip: There is no statutory definition of what an ETO reason is however it is likely to include:

(i) a reason relating to the profitability or market performance of the new employer's business (i.e., an economic reason);

(ii) a reason relating to the nature of the equipment or production processes which the new employer operates (i.e., a technical reason); or

(iii) a reason relating to the management or organisational structure of the new employer's business (i.e., an organisational reason).

Protection Against Dismissal For Transferring Employees

TUPE gives considerable protection to employees with more than 2 years' service against any dismissal by either the transferor or the transferee which is related to the transfer. Any dismissal of such an employee will be automatically unfair where the sole or principal reason for the dismissal is either:

- the transfer itself; or

- a reason connected with the transfer which is not an ETO reason.

The protection set out above under Regulation 7(1) of TUPE applies to any employee of the transferor or the transferee who is dismissed. It is not limited to transferring employees who are "assigned to the organised grouping of resources or employees" that is being transferred (*Regulation 7(4), TUPE*).

The effect of Regulation 7 is that the following employees are protected:

- those dismissed by the transferor prior to the transfer, whether or not they are employed in the undertaking or the part of it being transferred;

- those who remain employed by the transferor and do not transfer, but are subsequently dismissed by the transferor;

- those who transfer to the transferee under TUPE and are subsequently dismissed by the transferee; and

- those in the transferee's existing workforce who are dismissed as a result of the employment by the transferee of the transferring employees.

Dismissal by reason of the transfer itself

If the sole or principal reason for the dismissal is the transfer itself, the dismissal will be automatically unfair. There is no ETO defence. However, this situation will be extremely rare as the normal reason for dismissing employees will be to reduce the workforce numbers.

Dismissal for a reason connected with the transfer

Dismissals made before the transfer

Where an employee is dismissed before the transfer and is for an ETO reason, the liability for the dismissal will remain with the transferor.

Note that the transferor may not rely on the transferee's ETO.

Where a pre-transfer dismissal is by reason of the transfer or is connected with the transfer but is not for an ETO reason, then the dismissal will be automatically unfair and liability will transfer to the transferee, even if the employee was no longer employed at the time of the transfer (*Regulation 4(3), TUPE*) see ***Litster v Forth Dry Dock & Engineering Co Ltd [1989] IRLR 161.***

Dismissals following the transfer

If the dismissal is related to the transfer, then it will be automatically unfair unless the transferee can show an ETO reason. Liability will fall on the transferee.

There is no specific period after which dismissals will definitively not be connected with a TUPE transfer. However, the greater the time between the dismissal and the TUPE transfer, the more difficult it is for an employee to argue that there is a connection between the two.

Employee resignation: deemed dismissals

TUPE deems an employee's resignation to be a dismissal where it is in response to:

- An employer's repudiatory breach and the employee claims constructive dismissal (*Regulation 4(11) TUPE*);

- A substantial change to the employee's working conditions to their material detriment (*Regulation 4(9) TUPE*).

Employees who resign in these circumstances are treated as having been dismissed and are covered by Regulation 7 TUPE.

CHAPTER SEVEN

USING SETTLEMENT AGREEMENTS

Introduction

Settlement agreements can be a really useful tool in a corporate transaction. They can be used either by the transferor or the transferee at any stage during the transaction.

It is important to stress at this initial stage that they can offer some significant protection to the transferor or the transferee, knowing that if drafted correctly, they will protect them from subsequent litigation in the employment tribunal or the courts.

Essentially, when using a settlement agreement, it will mean that an employee is signing away their legal rights to pursue their statutory employment law rights. Therefore, there are some significant safeguards in place to protect employees. In this chapter we will explore those safeguards as well as some real-life practicalities of using these agreements during a corporate transaction.

What are settlement agreements?

A settlement agreement is a legally binding agreement, and in a corporate transaction usually involving the termination of employment either by the transferor or the transferee. The requirements for a valid settlement agreement are set out in s203(3) Employment Rights Act 1996 ("ERA 1996").

Various employment and anti-discriminatory legislation recognise a settlement agreement as an effective mechanism for settlement of a claim arising out of an employment dispute.

The requirements under s203(3) ERA are applied strictly and *all* the relevant requirements must be present, in order for the settlement agreement to be valid. Consequently, an agreement which fails to engage all the components of s203(3) will be invalid and unenforceable.

s203(3) Employment Rights Act 1996

(3) For the purposes of subsection (2)(f) the conditions regulating settlement agreements under this Act are that—

> *(a) the agreement must be in writing,*
>
> *(b) the agreement must relate to the particular proceedings,*
>
> *(c) the employee or worker must have received advice from a relevant independent adviser as to the terms and effect of the proposed agreement and, in particular, its effect on his ability to pursue his rights before an employment tribunal,*
>
> *(d) there must be in force, when the adviser gives the advice, a contract of insurance, or an indemnity provided for members of a profession or professional body, covering the risk of a claim by the employee or worker in respect of loss arising in consequence of the advice,*
>
> *(e) the agreement must identify the adviser, and*
>
> *(f) the agreement must state that the conditions regulating settlement agreements under this Act are satisfied.*

Practical tip: Ensure when you are drafting settlement agreements that you fully appreciate the section 203 requirements and that your drafting complies with all of these requirements. Failure to do so may make an agreement invalid!

The effect of a settlement agreement

The effect of a valid settlement agreement will be to waive an individual employee's *statutory* employment rights. These rights should be distinguished from either *common law* or *contractual rights*, which are capable of being waived in the absence of a settlement agreement. Statutory employment rights are those rights conferred by Parliament and which are enforceable in the employment tribunal. Examples relevant in a corporate transaction include:

- Unfair dismissal;
- Redundancy payments;

- Discrimination;
- Statutory minimum notice periods;
- Working time regulations;
- Unauthorised deduction from wages; and
- Minimum wage protection.

It is only on engagement of *all* the conditions specified in s203(3) ERA that a settlement agreement will operate so as to bar the jurisdiction of an employment tribunal to hear those statutory claims referred to in the agreement.

The terms of the settlement agreement often form the subject matter of negotiations between the parties. If the employment has already come to an end, care should be taken to ensure that negotiations do not progress beyond the limitation period for commencing an employment tribunal claim, without protective proceedings having been commenced.

<u>When would you use an agreement in a corporate transaction?</u>

Settlement agreements can either be used by a buyer or a Seller during the transaction. It may be that the Seller wishes to end the employment contracts, typically of senior executives, in order to make the business more attractive for sale.

Settlement agreements can also be used by the buyer once a transaction has taken place, either as part of a redundancy exercise or as part of renegotiating terms of contractual terms.

A buyer may also want to dismiss and re-engage on new terms and conditions. Within employment law principles, as we have seen under TUPE, the dismissal would be automatically unfair. The employee could argue that the dismissal was related to the transfer.

However, the transferee could seek to enter into a settlement agreement to resolve or prevent that claim from arising. The courts have approved the validity of using a settlement agreement in these circumstances. However, there is a risk that the employee could refuse the terms of a settlement agreement and exercise their right to pursue a claim of unfair dismissal in the employment tribunal. Clearly that is a commercial risk for the transferee during the course of a corporate transaction.

Practical tip: When taking client's instructions ensure that you take full details relating to the terms of the contractual arrangements, the history of the employment relationship and the full circumstances of bringing the employment relationship to an end.

Legal requirements

The agreement must be in writing

Section 203(3)(a) ERA provides that the agreement must be in writing. An oral agreement is not sufficient. The written document must set out the terms of the settlement agreement and identify the parties. The employee's full name and address should be specified. The correct employer must be identified and in the case of a corporate body, the company should be precisely specified.

Where an employee has been employed by a subsidiary company and negotiations leading up to the agreement have been conducted by the parent company, ensure that the right employer is named on the face of the agreement. Similarly, there are situations where a senior employee may have two employment contracts – one with a parent overseas company and another with a UK subsidiary company. It is important that both contracts are recorded in the settlement agreement.

Where an employer enters into a settlement agreement with a departing employee, consideration should be given to whether or not the agreement is also intended to settle any potential claims that the departing employee may have against third parties. The general rule is that only the parties to the agreement will be bound by its terms. However, the Contracts (Rights of Third Parties) Act 1999 has significantly reformed the privity of contract rule, giving third parties a right to enforce a term of a contract if the contract expressly provides for enforcement, unless on a proper construction of the contract it appears that the parties did not intend the term to be enforceable by the third party. Consequently, consideration should be given as to whether any waiver given in the settlement agreement is intended to operate for the benefit of third parties. It will often be the case that the agreement is drafted to include a waiver of claims against other group companies but there may also be instances where it is appropriate to seek a waiver of claims against trustees. ***(A F Blackmore and Son Limited and Others v Machin and Browne [2007] EWHC 963).***

The agreement must relate to the particular proceedings

Section 203(3)(b) ERA provides that the agreement must relate to the particular proceedings. Therefore, a settlement agreement made within actual proceedings must relate to *those* proceedings. Where an agreement is reached on the basis of anticipated proceedings, such proceedings should be specified. However, the agreement cannot be used to exclude potential complaints on the basis that they might arise at some later date (***Hinton v University of East London [2005] EWCA Civ 532***).

In order to be fully effective, settlement agreements must precisely identify the claims to be settled. A single settlement agreement may be used to settle more than one complaint, provided the agreement clearly identifies each of the complaints being compromised.

Ideally, all claims that an employee may reasonably have (both present and future) should be listed clearly and comprehensively in the settlement agreement (either by referring to the relevant statute or to a generic description) and then compromised. Even so, the agreement may not be effective to exclude potential complaints which have not yet arisen (***Hilton UK Hotels Ltd v McNaughton [2005] EAT/0059/04***).

Independent legal advice from a qualified adviser

Since the concept of a settlement agreement was first introduced in 1993 (when it was first referred to as a compromise agreement) it has been a basic requirement for such an agreement to be a fully valid settlement of a dispute between an employer and employee, that the employee must have had independent advice (see Employment Rights Act 1996 s.203(3), s 147(4) Equality Act 2010 and TULRCA 1992 s.288(2B)(c)).

Section 203(3)(c) ERA states that an employee must receive independent legal advice, from a "relevant independent adviser", about the terms and effect of the proposed settlement agreement and in particular its effect on the employee's ability to pursue his/her rights before an employment tribunal. If not, the agreement cannot be enforced by either party.

For the purposes of the above a "relevant independent adviser" is defined in S203(3A) as falling into one of the following categories:

- a qualified lawyer;
- an officer, official, employee or member of an independent trade union who has been certified in writing by the union as competent to give advice and as authorised to do so on behalf of the union;

- an employee or volunteer at an advice centre who has been certified in writing by the centre as competent to give advice and as authorised to do so on behalf of the centre; or
- a person of a description specified in an order made by the Secretary of State. Hence the Compromise Agreements (Description of Person) Order 2004 SI 2004/754 adds Fellows of the Institute of Legal Executives to this category.

It is common practice for larger employers to maintain a "list" of recommended solicitors, to whom employees are referred for the purposes of receiving advice on the settlement agreement. Payment for legal costs is then made direct to the solicitor after completion of the agreement. In principle there is nothing wrong with this practice as the solicitor is not acting in the matter for the employer or an associated employer.

Nevertheless, any solicitor that agrees to accept instructions by reference to recommendation from the employer's list, should ensure that s/he maintains his independence and that his/her advice to the employee is not influenced by virtue of the source of instructions. The *best interests* of the employee client will be paramount and, in any event, Rule 3.01 of the Solicitors Code of Conduct 2007 prohibits a solicitor from acting in circumstances where there is a potential conflict of interest.

The costs associated with independent legal advice

Over the years, a practice has developed where the outgoing employer makes a contribution towards the cost of legal advice given to the employer. As we have seen above, that is not a section 203 requirement. Therefore, if an employer does not make a contribution towards the employees associated legal costs it does not automatically make an agreement invalid.

However, in the balance of fairness, the practice has evolved where the employer will make a "contribution" towards the cost of the employee receiving legal advice. As a practitioner, we often stress that this is simply a *contribution* towards the overall cost, and doesn't automatically cover the full cost of the advice given, although the value of the contribution may well depend on the parties overall bargaining positions in the corporate transaction!

We have seen that the duties under section 203, as an independent relevant advisor, you are required to advise on the "terms and effect". This does not mean that an advisor has to provide independent advice on all aspects of all and any potential claims that the individual employee potentially has. In straightforward terms, it means that the employee has to be advised on the terms of the agreement, the nature of what they're signing and the implications of doing so – that by signing the agreement they are prevented from pursuing the claims that are listed in the body of the agreement.

In the useful case of ***Solomon and the University of Hertfordshire [2019] UKEAT 0258/18/2910*** HHJ Richardson considered the value of the financial contribution made by the employer. Here the employer had offered to pay £500 plus VAT to the claimant's independent advisor to allow the employee to seek advice on a settlement offer of £50,000. The University of Hertfordshire argued that this was sufficient consideration to cover all and any potential claims that Mr Solomon may have as part of the termination of his contract of employment. HHJ Judge Richardson disagreed at paragraph 110, stated that whilst £500+VAT might be enough to cover advice on the *"terms and effect"* of the proposed settlement agreement it was *"wholly unrealistic"* for a solicitor *"to advise on the merits of the Claimant's claim and the likely award of compensation"* for that amount, which *"would require reading and consideration on a quite different scale"*.

There must be in force a policy of insurance

Section 203(3)(d) ERA provides that there must be in force, when the advisor gives the advice, a contract of insurance, or an indemnity provided for members of a profession or professional body covering the risk of a claim by the employee or worker in respect of loss arising in consequence of the advice.

Clearly, this is an important aspect for solicitors giving advice on settlement agreements. In any event, it is a condition precedent for renewal of a practising certificate that the solicitor or his/her firm has in force an up-to-date policy of indemnity insurance which complies with the SRA's minimum terms and conditions. The provision of advice in the absence of either an up-to-date practising certificate and/or indemnity insurance, will have regulatory consequences.

The agreement must identify the adviser

Section 203(3)(e) ERA provides that the agreement must identify the adviser. The name and professional address of the particular "relevant independent adviser" must be stated within the settlement agreement. It is not sufficient merely to state the name of the adviser's firm or chambers.

The objective of ss203(3)(c) and 203(3)(e) is to protect the interests of an employee in ensuring that the third-party adviser is wholly independent and identified accordingly.

In *Sankyo Pharma (UK) Ltd v Bartlett (2000) EAT687/99*, the agreement contained no reference to the adviser. However, the adviser was identified in a covering letter attached to the agreement. The EAT held that the conditions under s203(3)(e) had on this occasion been satisfied as there was no authority requiring that the adviser's signature be inserted into the body of the agreement or that the agreement itself must only be in one document.

It is usual for an appropriately drafted settlement agreement to contain an "adviser's certificate", as an appendix to the agreement. The adviser's certificate will specify the name and address of the adviser and also contain a warranty as to the adviser's professional status, his/her firm and the fact that s/he is covered by a policy of indemnity insurance.

The relevant conditions must be stated as being satisfied

Section 203(3)(f) ERA provides that the agreement must state that the conditions regulating settlement agreements are satisfied. Hence if the parties are settling complaints under more than one statute, then all the precise statutory provisions should be identified.

In *Palihakkara v British Telecommunications plc (2006) UKEAT/0185/06)* the EAT held that the agreement did not conform to the Race Relations Act 1976 and the Sex Discrimination Act 1975. The agreement had to contain a clause stating that it had fulfilled the conditions required by these Acts in order to be a valid agreement. Whether the content of the agreement did actually fulfil those conditions was irrelevant. The absence of the necessary statement rendered the agreement invalid.

The tax position

Relevant legislation is contained in:

- Finance (No. 2) Act 2017
- Income Tax (Earnings and Pensions) Act 2003 ss.225-6 (formerly ICTA 1988 s.313)
- Social Security Contributions and Benefits Act 1992 s.4(4)(b)
- HMRC notes EIM12800 – Termination payments and benefits

Basic tax position

The basic tax position at the time of writing is that the first £30,000 paid under the terms of a settlement agreement is paid free of tax provided it is an *ex-gratia* (non-contractual) payment and is genuine consideration for entering into the agreement.

However, the £30,000 exemption does not apply if and to the extent that the cash sum is not in settlement of claims but is in return for other consideration, typically that the ex-employee is agreeing to be bound by new restrictive covenants. Almost invariably the ex-employee agrees not to sue the employer. That agreement not to sue is itself a form of restrictive covenant (regardless of any other restrictive covenants in the agreement) and therefore if any of the cash sum is attributable to that it will be taxable under Income Tax (Earnings and Pensions) Act 2003 ss.225-6.

> Practical tip: Be clear in your own mind on the value and amount of any ex-gratia severance payment and how it is to be calculated. When drafting make a clear distinction between the different elements i.e., itemising separate amounts for pay in lieu of notice, statutory redundancy payments and any ex-gratia payments.

It should also be noted that some ex-gratia payments to ex directors may require shareholder approval (and this may need to be dealt with as part of the completion steps) – see Chapter 10 for more information.

Main tax exemptions

It is important to remember that there are certain payments made on termination of employment during a corporate transaction which will not attract a charge to tax at all, either as employment income or under s401. In order to qualify, these payments must not be related to the termination payments. As such, these payments will fall outside the £30,000 exemption and do not have to be included when assessing the total value of the termination payment for the purposes of the exemption. The main payments relevant to lawyers in a corporate transaction are:

1. Injury to feelings compensation in discrimination claims: in claims for discrimination, in addition to any economic loss suffered by the employee, there will also often be a claim for injury to feelings. If the discrimination is found to occur before termination of employment, HMRC has accepted that any compensation attributable to that (including for injury to feelings) will be wholly exempt from tax; and

2. Payments on account of disability: under s406(2) ITEPA, neither tax nor NIC will apply to a payment made on account of an employee's injury or disability.

TAX FLAG: It is important to stress here that a practitioner should always seek separate tax advice on the nature of these types of payments. Your client may also want to seek clearance from the HMRC

Making payments

Outstanding wages, bonuses, commission and holiday pay are fully taxable, being payments made under the employee's contract of employment.

Ex gratia sums paid as compensation for loss of employment under the terms of the settlement agreement are taxable, but subject to the £30,000 tax-free exemption. This includes statutory and contractual redundancy payments, provided that they are made on account of genuine redundancy.

Where an employee receives a contractual payment in lieu of notice, the payment is chargeable to tax as earnings from employment. The distinction between contractual and non-contractual PILONs was removed in April 2018, meaning tax will be due on all payments equating to notice pay (The Finance (no 2) Act 2017).

With the employee's legal costs, no tax charge will be imposed on a payment made directly from the employer to the employee's solicitor as long as the payment is made pursuant to a specific term in the settlement agreement and the payment is in discharge of the solicitor's costs incurred solely in connection with the termination of the employee's employment.

TAX FLAG: If in doubt, employers should seek specific advice on the tax treatment of the various payments being made under the terms of an agreement and should include a tax indemnity from the employee in the agreement. This will mean that the primary liability for any unpaid tax will rest with the employee, although the employer would need to enforce the indemnity. Legal advisers acting for employees frequently request the removal of a tax indemnity clause, arguing that it is for the employer to take a view on the tax treatment of the payments at the time the agreement is entered into. This is entirely a matter for negotiation and one on which an employer will take its own view.

Practical tip: Ensure you are clear on the proposed termination date in an agreement and ensure any payments are included up to the proposed termination date.

Restrictive covenants and confidentiality obligations

Following a due diligence exercise it will be clear whether or not the protection contained in any restrictive covenants is adequate or not from the transferee's position. An employer wishing to restrict an employee from acting in competition, or soliciting customers or employees following a corporate transaction needs to give careful thought to their position.

Frequently contracts of employment contain no restrictive covenants whatsoever, or they are too wide to be legally enforceable. Therefore, the buyer may wish to amend the contracts of key employees so that they are able to rely on restrictive covenants. In doing so any buyer needs to be mindful of the implications of TUPE and harmonisation (see Chapter 11).

Clearly it will be in the buyer's interest to ensure that any settlement agreement relating to an executive's departure contains valid restrictive covenants that are either restated or new covenants entered into in order to protect the business moving forward. In the case where new covenants are entered into, adequate consideration needs to be provided to the outgoing employee.

It is important to allocate a payment as consideration in return for these new covenants, because of the general contract law requirement that a contract is not binding unless each party gives consideration. There is also an equitable principle that the court will not grant an injunction (the most common remedy in breach of covenants cases) unless consideration has been paid. This payment is fully taxable under sections 225 and 226 of ITEPA 2003 and liable to NICs.

It is also generally accepted that the length of any new restrictive covenants in a sale and purchase agreement will be longer than the period in which they would normally be in their contracts of employment or settlement agreement allowed under employment law principles. See Chapter 9 for further discussion surrounding restrictive covenants in the sale and purchase agreement.

Personal injury claims

The employer may wish to obtain a waiver from the employee of any personal injury claims. This could relate to:

- Claims that have already been brought.
- Existing claims of which the employee is not aware. There would appear to be no reason why such a waiver could not be effective, provided the wording is sufficiently clear
- Claims that have not yet arisen. **Such a waiver would not be effective since it would be an exclusion clause under UCTA.**

Pension claims

Under section 91 of the Pensions Act 1995, it is not possible to waive any accrued pension rights except in certain (limited) circumstances.

More importantly, any such rights are usually owed to the employee by the trustees of the pension scheme, who are not a party to the settlement agreement. The trustees would therefore not be bound by the terms of the settlement agreement and would be in breach of trust if they then failed to provide the employee with the benefits to which the employee is entitled under the pension scheme (***A F Blakemore and Son Ltd v Machin [2007] EWHC 963 (Ch) and Lewis v The Pensions Ombudsman [2005] EWHC 103***)

When drafting settlement agreements, employers should therefore consider if it is necessary to compromise claims against third parties (most commonly group companies, but also pension trustees). The potential claims against any third party should be clearly identified (see ***Naeem v BCCI [2002] 1 AC 251***). The Contracts (Rights of Third Parties) Act 1999 would give the third party the right to enforce any terms in the settlement agreement which purport to confer a benefit on them.

Claims that cannot be settled in a corporate transaction

It is not possible to settle a number of statutory rights by means of a settlement agreement. These include claims for failing to inform and consult or failure to pay the compensation that is equivalent to the protective award under the TUPE, as well as claims for failure to provide employee liability information under TUPE.

This is for clear public policy reasons. The spirit of TUPE is to inform and consult with those that are affected by the corporate transaction. Therefore, it is unpalatable for claims of this nature to be settled through an agreement and any clause in any agreement would therefore be invalid.

However, in practical terms the value of an ex-gratia payment to the outgoing employee is a huge incentive not to pursue these types of claims in the employment tribunal in any event.

CHAPTER EIGHT

SALE AND PURCHASE AGREEMENT

What should the document be called?

In practice, the acquisition agreement is often given a variety of abbreviations, so it is useful to clarify what each of these may be referring to:

- APA – Asset Purchase Agreement
- BPA – Business Purchase Agreement
- SPA – refers to either the Sale and Purchase Agreement or a Share Purchase Agreement.

Regardless of the abbreviation, they are all referring to the contract governing the corporate acquisition.

The key issue is to ensure you are clear on whether it is a share sale or asset sale (where the business is sold as a going concern) as noted in Chapter 3.

If you are responsible for preparing the first draft, it is vital to ensure you select the appropriate precedent which will depend on the choice of structure. A common error is to select a business purchase agreement when in fact you are advising on a share purchase.

In a private treaty sale, it is usual for the buyer's solicitors to produce the first draft of the sale and purchase agreement (which will therefore be more buyer friendly and have full warranties). In an auction sale, it is common for the Seller's solicitors to produce the first draft. This will therefore be likely to be more Seller friendly, have less warranties and stronger vendor protection clauses. See Chapter 9.

> Practical tip:
>
> When choosing an appropriate precedent, key issues to consider are:
>
> - Form of the Seller(s) (i.e., is it a company or an individual)?
> - Number of Sellers (for example, if there is only one Seller, using a precedent for multiple sellers is inappropriate as it will include statements such as "the Sellers jointly and severally…."). Remember to use your diagram of parties to assist when drafting.
> - Will there be simultaneous exchange or completion or will there be a split exchange and completion (see Chapter 10 for the additional considerations for a gap between exchange and completion)?
> - Will a short form agreement be appropriate (for example, due to the transaction being low risk or the value of the deal/risk appetite of the parties) or is a long form agreement required (long form provides lengthy warranties and additional buyer protections)?
> - Are you drafting a buyer friendly or seller friendly version?

<u>Structure of a share sale agreement</u>

The agreement usually contains the same key provisions which are as follows:

- Parties
- Definitions and interpretation
- Conditions precedent
- Agreement to sell the shares/purchase the shares
- Consideration (and relevant adjustment mechanism which depends on valuation process used)
- Process for completion (see Chapter 10)
- Buyer protections (see Chapter 9)
- Seller protections (see Chapter 9)
- Restrictive covenants (see Chapter 9)

- Boilerplate (including entire agreement clauses and governing law and jurisdiction
- Schedules, which may include:
    - o Warranties and tax indemnity (see Chapter 9)
    - o Completion mechanics (see Chapter 10)
    - o Pension arrangements
    - o Completion accounts process (see consideration analysis)
- Signatures/Execution block for each party

Additional clauses for an asset sale agreement

As noted in Chapter 3, the asset sale agreement will also contain additional clauses to reflect the change in structure, for example it will include a list of assets used in the business and included within the sale (and may also include a list of all assets excluded from the sale).

Chapter 6 details the additional employment issues that will need to be dealt with (and see below for other issues including TUPE specific indemnities).

In addition, the agreement should also include consideration allocation, a VAT clause, how third-party contracts and book debts will be dealt with, and any protections required by the buyer due to the likelihood that the Seller (the trading company) will be a cash shell post completion and is likely to transfer the consideration up to the shareholders and then be liquidated.

Common clauses

As noted above, there are common elements in a sale and purchase agreement and each of these clauses will be discussed in turn. Where the clause is only applicable on an asset sale agreement, this will be noted.

Parties

The parties are usually the buyer and the Seller(s). This is often straightforward as in practice, often one buyer is purchasing all the shares in the Target from one shareholder (whether they are an individual shareholder or a corporate shareholder).

As noted during the due diligence process, on a share sale, you must be clear from the outset who owns the shares in the Target. If there are multiple shareholders (and therefore more than one seller), the details of the each of the Sellers can be set out in a schedule to the agreement. Each of these shareholders must be a party to the agreement to be able to agree to sell their shares to the buyer (as well as entering into all of the buyer protections that are negotiated). This is a key reason why the practical tips above include making sure you are clear on the number of Sellers involved as there will be wording throughout the document that will need to be considered/amended (e.g., see joint and several liability discussion below).

If you do have multiple shareholders, you must not automatically assume that all of the Sellers are all bearing all of the liabilities under the sale and purchase agreement (for example, it may be not all of the Sellers will be giving the warranties).

There may be one or more of the Sellers who own shares but have no other role within the Target, and therefore have limited knowledge about the Target, which will usually translate as a reluctance to be liable for the warranties.

This could be a spouse of a Seller (or in a family company, some members may no longer be involved in the day to day running of the company). It could even simply be an investor who was happy to provide capital but has no actual involvement in the running of the company (such as a business angel). These are all examples of individuals who are likely to wish to avoid giving the warranties as they lack the requisite knowledge of the Target/business. There are other categories of investor who will also share this reluctance, such as trusts and venture capitalists – see "warranties and indemnities" section in Chapter 9 below for further discussion surrounding this issue.

The sale and purchase agreement must expressly set out how the Sellers' liabilities and obligations are shared (and the buyer will commonly request that the warranties and indemnities are given by all Sellers on a joint and several basis). This is often the standard position in a precedent for multiple Sellers, but you must check with your client what the actual agreed position is, based on the issues connected with joint Sellers above.

> Practical tip:
>
> Where there are multiple Sellers, check:
>
> - Does the agreement expressly have them all giving the warranties?
> - Is there additional wording expressly covering how they share liabilities (e.g., "unless expressly provided otherwise, the Sellers shall be jointly and severally liable for their obligations and liabilities under this agreement").

It is not common for the Target to be a party to the share purchase agreement (but if the buyer would like the Target to be able to enforce obligations, such as the restrictive covenants (see Chapter 9), you may consider amending the boilerplate clause relating to the Contracts (Rights of Third Parties) Act 1999 to allow the Target to enforce these obligations. This is similar to the discussion enabling the Target to enforce the Confidentiality/Non-Disclosure Agreement in Chapter 4.

There may also be additional parties based on the facts of the transaction (such as guarantors – if the guarantee is included within the sale and purchase agreement instead of a separate stand-alone document, the guarantor will need to be a party to the contract). As noted in Chapter 3, you must continue to use your diagram of the transaction to ensure all of the appropriate parties are included.

Definitions and interpretation

A definitions section is useful for clarity and avoids repetition throughout the contract. Two key definitions to check are the definition of "Warranties" and "Disclosed". See Chapter 9 for the issues to check in relation to these defined terms.

In addition, the interpretation clause is useful, but care must be taken to check it carefully. For example, the clause relating to statutory interpretation may deal with multiple Sellers (so it must be checked to ensure it reflects what has been agreed in relation to joint and several liability).

It may be if there is a reference to statutory provisions, the Seller(s) will not want it to include post completion amendments to the provisions. This is because there is a risk that it could increase their liability in relation to the warranties; if the Seller warrants all statutes have been complied with, if legislation subsequently becomes more stringent post completion (see practical tip box below).

> Practical tip: Check each clause carefully – Do not assume the interpretation/boilerplate is standard and should not be amended.
>
> For example, the Seller will not want references to statutory provision to include all subordinate legislation "*made from time to time*". It should ensure that it is only covering subordinate legislation made "*as at the date of the agreement*".

Conditions precedent

Ideally, the transaction will have a simultaneous exchange and completion. The issues arising where there is a gap between exchange and completion are set out in Chapter 10.

One of the most common reasons for requiring this gap is the need for conditions precedent to be satisfied. What this means is that the parties will execute the sale and purchase agreement (exchange) with completion being subject to the satisfaction of the conditions included in the sale and purchase agreement.

These conditions vary depending on the transaction but can include shareholder consent, HMRC clearance, UK Competition and Markets Authority clearance for UK transactions, regulatory consent or consent from other third parties (see third party contracts below).

When drafting the conditions, each condition must be defined so it is clear exactly what needs to be done and by whom. It must also set out a date when the conditions must be satisfied by and the consequences of failure to satisfy the condition by this date (e.g., if the condition is not capable of waiver, it may be that the agreement automatically terminates; or if the condition is capable of waiver, that the relevant party waives the condition prior to this date).

In addition to careful drafting of the conditions precedent, it must also be appreciated that the necessity for these conditions will result in a split exchange and completion, which carries additional risks for the buyer. See Chapter 10 for the additional methods the buyer will seek to utilise to address these risks.

Agreement to sell the shares/purchase the shares/business

This is a straightforward clause – the sale and purchase agreement must state exactly what is being purchased, i.e., the shares in the Target or the assets of the business. As noted above, on the sale of a business, it is usual to have a list of all of the assets that are being purchased together with a list of excluded assets.

Practical tip:

Ensure that the buyer will get good title to the assets being purchased. Things to be checked are:

- The shares are sold with full title guarantee and free from all encumbrances (such as securities, with all rights that attach to those shares (for example, dividends and voting rights);
- The Seller waives any pre-emption rights or any other restrictions that may impact the ability to transfer the shares to the buyer; and
- The buyer is not obliged to purchase the shares or assets unless all of the items for sale can be acquired simultaneously.

Consideration (and relevant adjustment mechanism which depends on valuation process used)

The purchase price is a key issue for the parties. It must clearly cover three key elements:

- Element 1: The amount (including whether the price is fixed or if it will be adjusted after completion based on either a debt free/cash free or net asset valuation);
- Element 2: The form the consideration will take (i.e., cash, shares in the buyer and/or loan notes (i.e., debt) from the buyer); and
- Element 3: The timing for payment (i.e., in full at completion or whether there will be some element of deferred consideration, e.g., payment by instalments, or a delay due to the requirement for completion accounts (see Element 1) or where an earn out is in place (see below)).

TAX FLAG: See Element 3. There are tax issues in relation to deferred payments that are outside the scope of this text.

Element 1 – Adjustment to the consideration

If the consideration is to be adjusted after completion, the sale and purchase agreement will need to set out the basis of the adjustment together with how the price was reached (e.g., on a net asset valuation or on a debt free/cash free basis).

Debt free/cash free can be visualised as the Target (or business) being a wallet – the buyer is purchasing the wallet on the basis that it is completely empty of cash and IOUs (i.e., the Seller will satisfy all debt and extract all cash from the Target/business before completion). Any cash or debt that remains within the wallet (the Target/business) will cause an adjustment to the consideration after completion.

To ascertain how much cash or debt is in the Target at completion will require accounts to be drawn up after completion (known as "**Completion Accounts**").

A schedule will be required to the sale and purchase agreement setting out the process of drawing up and agreeing these accounts. The adjustment to the consideration is usually set out as being on a pound for pound basis once the Completion Accounts process has been finalised.

An alternative to Completion Accounts is basing the consideration on old accounts which are known as "Locked Box" accounts. If these are used, there are benefits to both parties including the fact that time is not lost drawing up Completion Accounts post completion. However, there are also risks to both parties and care must be taken to agree between the parties what may leave the Target in the form of "authorised leakage" prior to completion (that the buyer will not receive any adjustment for) and what is "unauthorised leakage" where the Seller has taken value out of the Target after the date of the Locked Box accounts and prior to completion (such as unauthorised dividends). The Seller will usually be required to pay the buyer on a pound for pound basis for any unauthorised leakage that occurs.

Element 2 – Form of the consideration

Shares in the buyer will usually only be acceptable to the Seller as a form of consideration if the buyer if listed on a relevant investment exchange (such as the London Stock Exchange). This liquidity issue must be considered as if the buyer were a private company, the Seller would have difficulty in selling the shares in the buyer (and therefore may not achieve the full amount of consideration the Seller is expecting).

The Seller(s) objectives must also be considered – for example, if the Seller is entering into the corporate transaction due to a desire to exit the relevant market, it will be unlikely to want to acquire shares in the same market as part of the consideration for the transaction.

Loan notes issued by the buyer to the Seller(s) are usually for part of the consideration, and for tax reasons at the time of writing, cannot be repaid earlier than 6 months after completion. The loan note often has interest attached, but regardless of the fact the Seller may earn interest on the debt, there are risks attached to allowing the buyer to defer payment of part of the consideration, including the risk of the buyer going into insolvency (or bankruptcy if the Seller is an individual) and being unable to pay their debt (although this may be mitigated by securing the loan note against assets of the buyer). There are also potential tax benefits to accepting loan notes, but this must be balanced against the risks attached and the delay in receiving the consideration.

TAX FLAG: if paper consideration is contemplated as part of the consideration (e.g., shares/loan notes), tax advice must be taken.

Element 3 – Earn out?

An earn out is usually only relevant where there is an individual Seller who wishes to continue working in/for the Target/business after completion. The Seller will receive part of their consideration at completion, with the remaining part to be paid after completion of the transaction dependant on the profits the Target generates after completion.

An earn out means that the portion of deferred consideration is uncertain and is dependent on future performance. There will need to be an agreement as to how this future consideration is to be valued and paid (which is usually another schedule to the sale and purchase agreement).

The most common disputes post completion surrounding an earn out are usually as a result of the Seller(s) arguing the buyer has artificially or deliberately engineered the Target's performance to appear lower than reality or both parties disagreeing about the profit calculations. This can be dealt with by clearly setting out in the sale and purchase agreement how this is to be conducted.

TAX FLAG – deferred consideration may impact both parties tax position and tax advice must be taken prior to this arrangement being agreed.

Consideration allocation ***(asset sale only)***

As noted above, the consideration will be an agreed amount.

However, on the sale of a business as a going concern, each item being sold will be listed in the business purchase agreement and attached to each item must be an allocation of a proportion of the consideration.

The total will add up to the agreed consideration, but an amount must be set against each asset (and this is often included in a schedule to the agreement).

By doing this, you are setting the base cost of each individual asset for future disposals of those assets.

TAX FLAG: there are tax implications for both parties when agreeing these allocations and tax advice must be taken.

VAT (asset sale only)

As noted in Chapter 3, a share sale is VAT exempt. On the sale of a business as a going concern, VAT is potentially chargeable on the capital assets and stock. However, if the sale is a transfer of a business as a going concern, it is possible to utilise the exemption set out in Article 5 of the **VAT (Special Provisions) Order 1995 (SI 1995/1268)** to take the transaction outside the scope of VAT.

> Value Added Tax (Special Provisions) Order 1995
>
> 5—
>
> (1) Subject to paragraph (2) below, there shall be treated as neither a supply of goods nor a supply of services the following supplies by a person of assets of his business—
>
> (a) their supply to a person to whom he transfers his business as a going concern where—
>
> (i) the assets are to be used by the transferee in carrying on the same kind of business, whether or not as part of any existing business, as that carried on by the transferor, and
>
> (ii) in a case where the transferor is a taxable person, the transferee is already, or immediately becomes as a result of the transfer, a taxable person or a person defined as such in section 3(1) of the Manx Act....

To satisfy this exemption, the conditions in Article 5 must be complied with:

Condition (i) commentary

The assets purchased must be used by the buyer in the same kind of business as that carried on by the Seller with no significant break. This means in practice that the business carried out after completion must be a mirror image of what was conducted prior to completion without any changes. There is also no definition of how long this mirror image should be maintained before the business may be altered.

Condition (ii) commentary

The buyer must be or become registered for VAT.

<u>TAX FLAG: tax advice must be taken to ensure that the transaction falls within the Article 5 exemption.</u>

It should be noted from the analysis above in relation to condition (i) that there is always a risk that HMRC may deem the transaction does not fall within the Article 5 exemption and the sale and purchase agreement therefore needs to contain drafting to ensure the Seller(s) are protected from this risk.

To do this, the agreement must state that the consideration is exclusive of VAT. If this is not expressed, the consideration will be deemed inclusive of VAT and in the event HMRC rules that VAT is chargeable due to the failure of Article 5 to apply to the transaction, the Seller(s) will be liable to account for this. To address this risk, as well as expressly stating the consideration is exclusive of VAT, the agreement should also include an indemnity from the buyer to the Seller(s) to pay any VAT arising from the transaction.

Third party contracts (asset sale only)

It is vital that the buyer gets the benefit of all contracts it is intending to purchase from the Seller - it needs to acquire all the contracts that relate to the running of the business being purchased.

There are three methods of achieving this: by assignment, novation or negotiation of a fresh contract.

In relation to assignment, the relevant contract must be analysed to confirm whether there are any prohibitions on assignment or whether the consent of the third party is otherwise required. Regardless of this, assignment is not the preferable option for any key contract, as only the benefit of the contract can be assigned (e.g., receiving payment) and never the burden, which would remain with the Seller (e.g., to perform any obligations under the contract). Assignment is more common for smaller, less important contracts (and the buyer will usually agree in the sale and purchase agreement to perform these contracts on behalf of the Seller(s) and indemnify the Seller(s) in the event of any liability arising under such contracts).

Where the contract is key to the business, as noted above, assignment is not the best option. Novation or negotiation of a fresh contract avoid the issues connected with assignment.

Novation is a tripartite agreement between the buyer, the Seller(s) and the relevant third party, where the third party agrees to release the Seller(s) from any obligations under the contract and the buyer steps in to take over both the benefit and the burden of the contract. Similarly, the third party may agree to negotiating an entirely fresh contract with the buyer. Both methods involve the consent of the third party and will need to be taken into account when considering the timetable. It may be that the parties will agree to making completion conditional on the novation or execution of new key contracts which will require conditions precedent (see above) and a split exchange and completion (see Chapter 10).

Book debts and creditors (asset sale only)

Book debts represent money owed to the business by third parties (so are viewed as an asset of the business being sold). Creditors of the business are the opposite – this is money owed by the business to third parties. There are three options in relation to these assets and liabilities:

Option 1: transfer to the buyer;

Option 2: leave behind with the Seller(s); or

Option 3: leave behind with the Seller(s) but buyer collects debts in on behalf of the Seller(s).

Option 1

If the buyer elects to take on the debtors and creditors, these must be clearly specified in the asset purchase agreement (and appropriate steps taken to ensure they are assigned to the buyer). Before the buyer decides on acquiring these, they should consider the pros and cons to this approach.

One key drawback to the buyer acquiring debts is the risk that they may never be paid (and therefore become bad debts). Even if they are paid off in full, they will not be paid immediately (as will be repaid according to their agreed terms) and therefore also cause a practical cash flow issue to the buyer. It may be that the buyer will attempt to agree to acquire these debts at a discounted rate to address these risks, although agreeing the discount may be commercially difficult to achieve (and the buyer will usually ask for additional warranties in relation to the debts etc.).

Regardless of the risks above in relation to acquiring the debts/taking on the creditors, one of the main incentives for the buyer to do so is to negate the risk of the Seller pursuing repayment of these debts aggressively/delaying paying its own outstanding debts. Both actions have the potential to damage future goodwill with these third parties (who may include suppliers, customers and other creditors) who, after completion, will be in an ongoing relationship with the buyer.

Option 2

An issue for the Seller in relation to this option is a purely practical issue - if it has sold the entire business of the trading company (and has no other retained divisions etc.), it may not be able to actually collect in any debts (e.g., if all of the employees who would have previously collected in outstanding debts/paid bills etc. have transferred to the buyer as noted in Chapter 6).

Option 3

This is often the practical compromise – the creditors and debtors are left behind with the Seller(s), but the buyer agrees to collect in the debts as the agent of the Seller(s) (potentially for a fee or a percentage of the debts collected, which has the added benefit of providing an additional incentive to the buyer). This operates to give the Seller a method of collection whilst allowing the buyer to maintain good ongoing relationships with the third parties.

Boilerplate (including entire agreement clauses and governing law and jurisdiction

As noted above, the boilerplate is fundamental and must be carefully reviewed and amended where appropriate. It is vital to clarify whether the parties have decided to use alternative dispute resolution in the event of any disputes under the agreement and where the governing law and jurisdiction is to be located, and this must be reflected in the drafting.

Execution block for each party

Care must be taken to ensure the agreement is signed correctly by each party to the sale and purchase agreement. If there is any question as to whether consideration is being given by each party in relation to the restrictive covenants (and any indemnities), it may be that the agreement will be signed as a deed.

The correct execution block for each party must be selected and you must ensure that the correct parties are signing the document (for example, where a party is a company, a certified copy of the board resolution authorising the relevant person(s) to sign the documentation must also be provided).

CHAPTER NINE

THE RISK APPORTIONMENT GAME

Overview

Both the Seller(s) and the buyer wish to protect themselves from the risks associated with the transaction. The buyer will be worried about risks inherent in acquiring the Target or the business and the Seller(s) ideally are looking for a clean break on a share sale where they have sold the Target and in both a share sale and an asset sale, wish to be free to use the consideration however they see fit. A prudent Seller, knowing they may be held liable for future breach of warranty/indemnity claims for a certain number of years after completion, would potentially not feel free to use the consideration as they wished until the risks had passed.

The contractual protections negotiated in the sale and purchase agreement are aimed at giving each party the comfort they are seeking. It can be seen as a risk apportionment game – with every item negotiated, the risk is being moved from one side to the other. It will turn on bargaining power where the risk ends up remaining and each party has a variety of options at its disposal which will be looked at in turn.

Buyer's protection

Warranties and indemnities

These are key protections for the buyer, but it is important to note that whilst they may be discussed together (and in practice are often referred to together), they are very different protections with different roles and will be looked in turn.

Warranties

A warranty is a contractual statement of fact about the Target or the business the buyer is acquiring.

Warranties have a dual purpose – the first is that if the warranties are untrue at completion, the buyer has the ability (subject to the usual rules on breach of contract such as remoteness/reasonable foreseeability etc.) to pursue the Seller(s) for a breach of contract claim and damages.

A breach of contract claim aims to put the buyer in the position they would have been in if the warranty had not been breached/untrue. This is very difficult to prove in relation to a share sale, as the buyer would need to demonstrate the value of the Target has decreased as a result of the breach. As with any breach of contract claim, the buyer will also have to mitigate their loss for any breach of warranty claim.

Due to these difficulties in relation to succeeding in a claim for breach of warranty, the second purpose of the buyer seeking warranties is to trigger disclosures from the Seller(s) about the Target/business. See the Seller(s) protections below for more information about disclosures.

The buyer will wish to seek warranties about all of the information relevant to the Target/business (such as contracts, clients, IP, employees, litigation etc.) together with any items the buyer has found out about in due diligence that they wish to be contractually reinforced (e.g., if there is something they wish to rely on).

As noted in Chapter 8, the buyer usually prepares the first draft of the sale agreement on a private treaty sale and will therefore aim to include a wide raft of warranties to cover all their concerns. Example warranties are that there is no litigation in the Target, that the Target has complied with all applicable legislation and no key clients have served written notice that they intend to terminate the contract. The warranties are usually grouped into categories such as corporate, commercial, finance, tax, employees etc.

Once the buyer has circulated the warranties, the Seller(s) will review and amend them. See Seller(s) protections below for how the Seller(s) will approach these warranties.

Indemnities

An indemnity is a promise by the Seller to reimburse the buyer if a specific liability arises in the future. The key point to note is that the reason it is different to a warranty is that it is not a breach of contract claim – it is an action in debt (which means the common law rules relating to remoteness, mitigation etc do not apply). The whole purpose of the indemnity is to pay the buyer on a pound for pound basis for the actual loss suffered.

The buyer would seek indemnities for specific issues that have been disclosed to them. This illustrates the risk apportionment game – the buyer seeks warranties and therefore acquires protection, the Seller(s) disclose against the warranties in relation to specific issues (and therefore reduces the buyer's protection under the warranties). Once the buyer is aware of issues that have been disclosed, it can then choose to seek other commercial protections to address these specific risks (see "other commercial protections below).

Who gives the warranties and indemnities?

As noted above, it should not be automatically assumed that all the Sellers (assuming there is more than one) will all give the warranties and indemnities (for example, as discussed earlier, a minority shareholder may, quite rightly, not wish to assume the risks of a breach of contract claim connected with giving the warranties). However, where there is more than one Seller, the buyer will want each Seller to give all the contractual protections (on a joint and several basis). Joint and several liability means the buyer potentially can sue any one of the Seller(s) for the entire amount of the claim at hand.

In addition to minority shareholders discussed in Chapter 8, there is frequently negotiation around who gives the warranties and indemnities. For example, there may be a scenario where some shares are held by a trust or a private equity firm who have not been involved in managing the Target or business at all. Private equity firms are reluctant to give warranties when they sell a portfolio company as it then limits their ability to distribute funding to other proposed investments (as noted, a prudent Seller retains consideration to cover future liabilities). In a sale by a private equity team, their preference is that the "Warrantors" (see below) are the management team who are required to give all of the operational warranties. It is usually accepted in practice that whilst the private equity firm will not wish to give any operational warranties, they usually consent to give warranties that go to the heart of the transaction (for example, on a share sale, it is reasonable to insist that any private equity Sellers warrant they have good title to the shares and can freely sell them).

Certain shareholders may have a firm policy/ be under contractual terms (such as a trust deed) that may prevent them from giving warranty or indemnity protection and this can cause practical difficulties, so it is important that the identity of the warrantors is clear from the outset.

Practical tip:

If not all of the Seller(s) are going to be giving the warranties and indemnities, care needs to be taken with the definitions.

Instead of the Seller(s) warranting, there will be an alternative definition of "Warrantors", and this must only be used where not all of the Seller(s) are taking on the contractual liabilities under the sale and purchase agreement. Wherever the terms are used throughout the sale and purchase agreement, this must be checked to ensure it is referring to the intended parties.

In addition to ensuring the definitions are correctly dealt with, if more than one Seller is giving the warranties and indemnities, care also needs to be taken as to how they agree to share any risks and liabilities.

The Civil Liability (Contributions) Act 1978 allows any Seller who is liable to seek to recover a contribution from the other Seller(s) who are also liable for the claim.

Civil Liability (Contributions) Act 1978

Entitlement to contribution.

(1) Subject to the following provisions of this section, any person liable in respect of any damage suffered by another person may recover contribution from any other person liable in respect of the same damage (whether jointly with him or otherwise).

Assessment of contribution.

(2) Subject to subsection (3) below, in any proceedings for contribution under section 1 above the amount of the contribution recoverable from any person shall be such as may be found by the court to be just and equitable having regard to the extent of that person's responsibility for the damage in question.

As illustrated by the extract from the statute above, section 2 shows that if it is left to the court, the court will decide how much contribution this will be on a just and equitable basis. This is usually linked to how much consideration is received i.e., it would clearly not be just and equitable to make a minority shareholder who only received 10% of the consideration to be liable for 50% of the damages.

To avoid leaving this in the court's domain, the parties should specifically agree in writing how they will share the risks and liabilities. This could either be in the sale and purchase agreement or in a separate deed (often known as a deed of contribution). Key elements included should be the ratio in which the Warrantors will apportion the liability, how negotiations will be conducted/the decision-making process and any other procedural issues between the Warrantors themselves, such as consulting with each other on the progress of claims etc.

Regardless of what the Seller(s) agree between themselves, the buyer is still free to sue any (or all) of the Warrantors.

Representations

Historically, the Seller(s) were often asked to both "*represent and warrant*" in the sale and purchase agreement (and a prudent Seller would strongly resist the "representation" element). If this wording is retained, the Seller(s) would essentially be making representations about all the warranties.

A representation is a statement of fact that they buyer has relied on, and it induces them to entire into the sale and purchase agreement (and will be a misrepresentation if it is not true). The key issue behind representations is that it gives a different remedy in the event of a breach. As noted above, a successful breach of warranty claim would give rise to damages. A successful misrepresentation claim can also give rise to damages (which may be wider than breach of contract damages) but more importantly, may allow the buyer to rescind the contract. Recission effectively cancels the sale and purchase agreement from the beginning (which means it is treated as never having been entered into/existed).

The case of ***Idemitsu Kosan., Ltd v Sumitomo Corporation [2016] EWHC 1909 (Comm)*** clarified the position. In this case, the buyer was not able to pursue a warranty claim (due to being outside the time limits agreed in the sale and purchase agreement (see vendor protection clauses below for explanation and discussion surrounding time limits)) and instead sought to bring a claim in misrepresentation. This case would not have arisen if the buyer could have brought a breach of warranty claim and illustrates how important the vendor protection clauses can be.

The case suggested that the courts will not usually interpret warranties as also amounting to representations. If a party wishes to ensure they have an action for misrepresentation after completion, the agreement should clearly state any breach of warranty may also be a claim for misrepresentation. Reverting back to the risk apportionment "game", it would be unlikely for Seller(s) to agree, and a prudent Seller should insist that any item that the buyer is relying on to enter into the agreement should be made a warranty in the sale and purchase agreement (so that there is no issue in relation to pre contract representations). This will be reinforced by the Seller(s) requiring an effective entire agreement clause (which is another vendor protection clause discussed below).

TUPE specific indemnities

In a BPA, TUPE issues will normally be addressed, and an important number of indemnities are needed to be included against all claims, costs, expenses etc. incurred. This could be because of:

- The transferor's failure to comply with employment law pre-transfer;
- The transferor's failure to comply with its obligations under TUPE; and/or
- The automatic transfer of undisclosed employees or collective agreements because of TUPE.

  In these circumstances the buyer will want to reserve the right to terminate the employment contracts of those employees, or to terminate the collective agreements and will then in turn ask the Seller(s) to indemnify them in respect of costs and claims associated with such termination. The buyer will also want the option not to end the contract of employment or collective agreement and for the Seller(s) to indemnify them in respect of those ongoing contracts of employment.

- The transferee may also wish to seek an indemnity from the transferor in respect of post transfer liabilities as well as failing to inform and consult with transferring employees. This is of particular importance when you consider the obligations of joint and several liability. Indemnities may also be required covering any claims from transferring employees including constructive dismissal under Regulation 4(9) on the basis of proposed changes to their terms and conditions.

Other commercial protections (guarantees/retention accounts)

As noted above, there are many practical issues in terms of bringing a successful claim for breach of warranty (including mitigation, proving loss) and the Idemitsu case illustrated the vendor protection clauses (see below) can cause a valid breach of warranty claim to be "timed out" removing the appropriate avenue of redress (and in such cases, forcing the buyer to attempt to bring alternative claims to court to seek redress, often unsuccessfully).

To aim to reduce the buyer's risk, they should also consider other commercial and practical protections such as:

- Price reduction
- Restructuring
- Retention account
- Guarantees
- Restrictive covenants

These do not have to be utilised in isolation and can be used in combination with others (together with the warranties and indemnities). Each will be discussed in turn.

Price reduction

In the event the buyer discovers issues that impact the value of the transaction, in practice, this often triggers renegotiation of the consideration. As noted in Chapter 4, even if a price is agreed in the heads of terms, it is perfectly acceptable to negotiate a reduction in the event of matters disclosed. It may be considered preferable to deal with issues up front in this manner instead of risking a future indemnity claim, which the Seller(s) may not have the funds to pay (although this may be addressed by a retention – see below).

Restructure the transaction as an asset sale

Looking back at the key differences between a share sale and an asset sale discussed in Chapter 3, in the event there are liabilities 'lurking' in the Target, a buyer who still wishes to proceed with the transaction may wish to consider restructuring the transaction as an asset sale in order to purchase the assets of the business and leave the liabilities behind. This is a common way of continuing to pursue the transaction when a pension deficit in an occupational pension scheme is discovered – on a share sale, this s.75 Pensions Act liability remains with the Target, but on an asset sale, this liability would stay with the Seller.

This approach of restructuring will only work if the buyer does not wish to acquire a particular asset that retains the liability (for example, in the event of environmental contamination of a property, even if the transaction is restructured as an asset sale, this liability can only be left behind if the buyer chooses not to acquire that particular property). If the property was transferred, the buyer could still end up inheriting the liability for clean up on the basis that they are the current owner/occupier.

Retention account

One concern a buyer may have (particularly on an asset sale where the Seller will be a cash shell after completion) is that the consideration will be dissipated (as it will most likely be passed up to the shareholders of the Seller either by way of dividend or liquidation of the Seller i.e., the trading company) and there will be no monies left to pay the buyer in the event of a breach of warranty and/or indemnity claim.

To address this concern, the parties may agree that a proportion of the consideration is set aside in a retention account (which is usually simply a joint bank account operated between the buyer's solicitors and Seller(s)' solicitors. These monies are therefore ring fenced in the event the buyer is successful in a breach of warranty and/or indemnity claim.

The sale and purchase agreement should deal with what happens when any interest accrues on these monies and the length of time they will be retained in the joint account for (and usually these are linked to the time limits negotiated in the sale and purchase agreement).

Guarantees

It may be that the buyer wishes a third party to guarantee the Seller(s) liabilities under the sale and purchase agreement. This is more common again in respect of the sale of a business as a going concern where the Seller (which was previously the trading company prior to selling its assets) will be a cash shell after completion (and the buyer will commonly ask for the shareholders of the Seller for a guarantee.

Restrictive covenants

The buyer is either purchasing the entire Target (including its goodwill) or the business of the Target (including its goodwill). It is therefore absolutely acceptable for the buyer to require the Seller(s) to enter into restrictive covenants in order to protect its investment. If the Seller(s) were permitted to sell the Target or the business of the Target, and then set up a new company/business conducting exactly the same business as the Target after completion, this would clearly have a negative impact on the goodwill of the Target.

A restrictive covenant is a restraint of trade and as such, is unenforceable unless it is required to protect a legitimate business interest and is reasonable (in terms of scope, geography and time). It is clear there is a legitimate business interest to protect on the basis of the acquisition but in terms of reasonableness, the buyer must take care with the drafting to ensure that these covenants are enforceable after completion.

It is common to adopt the "blue pencil test" with restrictive covenants and ensure each restriction is a stand-alone restriction that, in the event it is struck out for lack of reasonableness, will not impact the remainder of the restrictions.

The covenants usually cover not competing with the Target/business, not soliciting customers or clients who have dealt with the Target/business for a set period of time, not soliciting key employees (as defined) for a set period of time after completion, not to use any confidential information about the Target (this does not need to be a finite period) and not to use the name of the Target (see completion list in Chapter 10 which often includes a special resolution for a change of name of the Seller on an asset sale to ensure the goodwill in the trading company name is purchased by the buyer).

In terms of the set period of time, this must be reasonable (and is usually between one and five years) and is judged transaction by transaction. Likewise, in respect of business scope and geography, the restrictions should be clearly linked to the current business scope (e.g., only restricting activities that the business or Target currently operate) and only looking at the area that the Target operates in, ensuring that this is reasonable.

Seller's protection

The Seller(s) are selling the Target/business in return for Consideration. As discussed above in relation to the buyer's protection, they will be giving contractual protections to the buyer. Although when you sell a company, in theory it is a clean break, the Seller(s) will still have ongoing contractual liabilities they owe to the buyer under the sale and purchase agreement.

In practice, the Seller(s) can limit their risk in three ways (and all of these methods can be used in conjunction with each other):

1. Negotiate the warranties
2. Disclose against the warranties
3. Utilise Vendor Protection clauses

Negotiate the warranties

One of the Seller(s) risk apportionment methods is to reduce the scope of the warranties (thereby both reducing the risk of future breach of warranty claims and also reducing the remit of disclosure (see below).

The Seller(s)' solicitors will approach the warranty schedule in three ways. They will firstly delete any warranties that are either not relevant to the transaction (such as stock warranties where stock is not forming part of the transaction) and will also delete any warranties that are outside of the Seller(s)' control (such as post completion occurrences for example the Seller(s) cannot warrant that no key clients will terminate after completion or that none of the key employees will leave after completion).

They will then negotiate the remaining warranties to ensure their remit is as narrow as possible (e.g., if accounts are being warranted, the number of years they will wish to warrant will be as small as possible – the buyer may ask for three years of accounts warranties, the Seller(s) may reduce this to the current year)). This narrowing serves two purposes – the first is to reduce the potential for breach as the scope of the warranty will be smaller and therefore harder to breach and the second is to make the disclosure process easier (as there will be less to disclose against).

Disclosure

Disclosure is a vital shield to a breach of warranty claim. If the Seller(s) successfully disclose against a particular warranty for a particular issue, they cannot be sued for a breach of warranty in relation to that particular issue. (As noted above, this is a key trigger in the risk apportionment game, as it is at this point the buyer will seek additional protection in the form of indemnities or price reduction etc.).

The disclosure letter is a simple letter from the Seller(s)' solicitors to the buyer's solicitors (usually negotiated by a junior in the team), attaching the disclosure bundle (which will be copies of all of the documentation relating to the disclosures e.g., accounts, contracts, litigation) (the "**Disclosure Bundle**"). This bundle must be compiled in relation to the disclosure letter regardless of the fact the buyer will have most likely been given access to these documents already in the data room.

The letter is in two parts – the general disclosures (often called the "*front end*") and the specific disclosures (often called the "*back end*").

General disclosures, if they are accepted by the buyer, are deemed to qualify the warranties. They usually take the form of matters that are part of public record (such as Companies House and Intellectual Property and Land Registry searches). They should be negotiated carefully as whatever is accepted by the buyer will qualify the warranties (regardless of whether the buyer has actually carried out the searches).

Specific disclosures are different and relate to specific warranties for example, disclosing that the Target is involved in litigation against the "no litigation" warranty. It is the specific disclosures that flush out additional issues for the buyer and lead to the buyer seeking additional protections such as indemnities.

The sale and purchase agreement will contain a clause that specifies the disclosures qualify the warranties.

There is no set standard of disclosure that must be achieved in order to qualify the warranties. The case of ***Infiniteland Ltd v Artisan Contracting Ltd [2005] EWCA Civ 758*** stated that the standard of disclosure must be set out in the contract – if the sale and purchase agreement only states "*the* warranties are qualified by matters disclosed", it is likely that vague, wide, unspecific disclosures could serve to qualify the warranties. However, if the sale and purchase agreement require "fair" disclosure, the standard the disclosure must be to achieve to qualify the warranties is raised. The case of ***MAN Nutzfarhzeuge AG and others v Freightliner Limited [2005] EWHC 2347 (Comm)*** supports this and reiterates the court will look at the standard of disclosure agreed between the parties and drafted in the sale and purchase agreement.

> Practical tip:
>
> When acting for the buyer, it is vital to check the wording in the sale and purchase agreement – it is common to see within the definitions section (or in the paragraph surrounding disclosure itself that "matters will be fairly, fully, clearly and accurately disclosed (with sufficient details to identify the nature and scope of the matters disclosed in the disclosure letter".

As noted above, raising the standard to fair is not controversial so should be expected by the Seller(s) and if the wording is raised to "fair", old case law is extremely useful to illustrate the level of detail that disclosure should go into in order to effectively qualify the warranties.

The key is to give the buyer specific notice of the issue the Seller(s) wish to disclose, ensuring that positive statements (and not omissions) are made (see case law example below); merely referring to an issue is insufficient.

The Seller(s) should not object to providing full disclosures and it is important to be clear with the Seller(s) that the more specific and detailed the disclosure, the more likely it will be to ensure that the applicable warranty is qualified and therefore provides them protection from a breach of warranty claim.

> Case law example illustrating "fair":
>
> ***Daniel Reeds Ltd v EM ESS Chemists Ltd [1995]*** related to a transaction selling a pharmaceutical company. The standard for disclosure was set at "fairly disclosed". The seller in this transaction gave a warranty that the target had valid licences for its products and the licences were set out in the schedule. The schedule accurately omitted a licence that the target did not have.
>
> It was not fair disclosure to just omit a key licence – the seller should have disclosed specifically that this key licence was missing.

As well as setting the standard for disclosure in the sale and purchase agreement, the Infiniteland case also clarified that the document must also state whether or not the buyer can pursue the Seller(s) post completion for breach of warranty when the buyer knew pre-completion about this breach. If the sale and purchase agreement say they can sue, then they will be able to bring a claim, if it says they cannot, then this will prohibit the claim. If the agreement is silent, then they may be able to pursue a claim.

A prudent buyer who knows about a breach of warranty claim prior to completion should be advised to deal with this issue up front (e.g. by way of price reduction, indemnity etc.) as despite the technical contractual ability to pursue a claim in the courts, the courts will not look favourably on this behaviour and may penalise a buyer on costs (particularly if the buyer has already received some form of adjustment to the purchase price based on this issue).

Vendor Protection clauses

Even with the reduced/negotiated warranties and disclosure, there will always be a risk of ongoing liability, therefore the Seller(s) will also request a number of limitation of liability clauses that will limit their liability (and these will be negotiated in the same way as the rest of the sale and purchase agreement).

Common vendor protection clauses are set out below.

Cap on liability

This is also known as a de maximus clause. Without this clause, the Seller(s) could potentially be liable for any amount (subject to the usual contractual rules on proving loss and the time limits under the Statute of Limitations (see below)). The Seller(s) will never want to be liable for more than they receive as consideration (and if their bargaining power is strong, may even try and set the cap for less than this). A cap on liability is not usually controversial but the buyer must consider whether they are comfortable having this cap apply to both the warranties and the indemnities (or solely the warranties). Care must be taken to check the definitions that apply to this clause very carefully.

Minimum claims

In the same way as the Seller(s) could be liable for large sums, without a minimum claims clause, they could also be liable for very small, inconsequential claims. The clause to prevent this is known as a de minimus clause – the aim is to prevent the Seller(s) being pursued for small or frivolous claims. This clause can be divided into two parts, an individual de minimus and an aggregate de minimus.

The individual de minimus will prevent a buyer from ever bringing a claim that is worth less than the amount set. In practice it is usually between £5,000 - £15,000 and can be considered the "throw away amount". Essentially, until a claim exceeds the throwaway amount, it cannot be counted in achieving the aggregate de minimus described below.

The aggregate de minimus prevents the buyer from bringing a claim unless the aggregate of those claims exceeds the amount agreed – this is usually around 1% of the consideration.

As with all of the vendor protection clauses, the drafting should be carefully considered. The Seller(s) position will be that they will only wish to be liable for any claims exceeding the agreed aggregate de minimus. The buyer's position will be that, whilst they will accept the aggregate de minimus, once the amount of a claim exceeds the value agreed, the Seller(s) should be liable for the entire amount. As with all negotiating, this outcome will depend on the bargaining power of the parties.

Time limits

Under the Statute of Limitations, the Seller(s) may be liable for a breach of contract claim for six years if the sale and purchase agreement is signed as a simple contract, or for twelve years if it is executed as a deed. As noted at the outset in Chapter 9, a prudent seller will be reluctant to spend the consideration until the risk has lapsed, therefore it is common in practice to agree a shorter period for the Seller(s) to be liable under the sale and purchase agreement.

For any non-tax claims, a common commercial practice is to agree a time limit of between one to three years. The Seller(s) would clearly prefer one year, and the buyer would prefer three – the general reasoning is that permitting two full audit periods should be sufficient to flush out any issues that would cause a breach of warranty.

For any tax claims, the reasoning is different than for non-tax claims. This is because HMRC can investigate the transaction for longer than this. Historically, HMRC were able to bring a claim in relation to the transaction for up to six years from the end of the accounting period from which the tax liability was incurred (and this time limit is still applicable in the event of careless behaviour). The time limit has now been reduced to four years (other than for careless behaviour as noted above or fraud or negligence) but despite this reduction, for this historic reason, it is common to see in sale and purchase precedents (and accepted) to permit the claims for breach of tax warranty (and under the tax indemnity) to be set at six years from the end of the Target's current accounting period (or seven years from the date of completion).

Entire agreement clause

As noted above pursuant to Idemitsu Kosan Co Ltd v Sumitomo case, a prudent Seller will not wish to be the subject of a misrepresentation claim (and will ensure the warranties are not also representations). To reinforce this, they will also require an effective entire agreement clause to confirm the sale and purchase agreement contains all of the terms agreed, and which will include five elements:

- Element 1 – The first statement will be an express statement that the terms in the sale and purchase agreement comprise all of the terms of the contract. Example wording is usually that "*the parties agree this agreement constitutes the entire agreement between the parties*". It should also ideally state it supersedes any other agreements between the parties.

- Element 2 – The second statement is usually a non-reliance clause confirming that the parties have not relied on any representations or other statements in entering into the contract (and should ensure that it covers any pre-contractual representations).

- Element 3 – The third statement is an express exclusion of liability for misrepresentation.

- Element 4 – The fourth statement should restrict the remedies to breach of contract only – the aim of this element is to ensure that the buyer cannot rescind (and to ensure that the damages solely relate to a breach of contract claim to remove the risk of wider damages for misrepresentation as noted above).
- Element 5 – The fifth statement should provide confirmation that the clause does not exclude liability for fraud. This is vital, as without it, it may lead to the court ruling the clause is ineffective due to lack of reasonableness.

> Practical tip:
>
> When drafting an entire agreement clause, use a precedent. It is very important to be aware that a shorter form entire agreement clause may not be effective and if you act for the Seller(s), it is vital to check all of the relevant components are included to ensure this is binding.

Other vendor protection clauses

There are usually other vendor protection clauses included such as requiring the buyer to pursue other third parties or insurance where possible prior to pursuing the Seller(s) for breach of warranty, and asserting the buyer can only claim once for damages (where there may be breach of more than one warranty).

In addition, the Seller(s) may wish to negotiate conduct of any claims that the Target is conducting or involved in that may result in the Seller(s) having to pay the buyer (e.g., for breach of warranty or under an indemnity). For example, if the Seller(s) have warranted that the Target has complied with its key contracts, if the Target is then successfully sued for breach of contract, the Seller(s) will be in breach of warranty and the buyer has a claim against the Seller(s). The same issue is relevant if the Seller(s) have provided an indemnity for the damages/costs incurred if they lose litigation. The Seller(s) will want to control the litigation on the basis that if the Target loses, it will be the Seller(s) who suffer the loss (and as the buyer knows they will have a claim against the Seller(s), they may be more likely to agree a settlement/not defend the claim as stringently). The buyer however may be concerned the Seller(s) conduct may impact on goodwill/reputation; therefore the parties may come to a practical agreement where one party may control the litigation with consent from the other etc.

Finally, the Seller(s) also have the option in addition to these measures agreed in the sale and purchase agreement, to take out warranty and indemnity insurance (although it should be noted that the both the premiums and the excess may be so high as to be prohibitive).

CHAPTER TEN

FINISHING THE DEAL

Simultaneous exchange and completion

As noted above in Chapter 3, a simultaneous exchange and completion is usually preferable. This provides certainty that the deal will proceed (for example, no party has changed their mind and all consents required have been obtained prior to the exchange and completion date). It also removes the risks to the buyer in relation to the gap between exchange and completion (see below).

In practical terms, "**exchange**" can be defined as the point where the sale and purchase agreement is executed by both parties (and the disclosure letter is delivered). At this point the parties are bound to complete the purchase (subject to any conditions precedent that are required to be satisfied).

"**Completion**" can be defined as when all of the formalities are concluded (for example, on a share sale, this would be the buyer paying the consideration to the Seller(s) and the Seller(s) delivering to the buyer an executed stock transfer form per shareholder for the shares in the Target).

What actually happens at exchange and Completion?

The parties should agree in advance whether Completion will be live or virtual.

Historically, all of the parties and their advisors used to gather in a meeting room (often at one of the solicitors' offices – usually the buyer's solicitors) to sign all of the documentation and finalise the completion process (including holding the Target board meeting).

All of the documents would be laid out on a long meeting room table often with different coloured post-it notes indicating who needed to sign where (which would then be removed after the solicitors had ascertained the correct parties had signed in the correct places), the necessary board meetings would take place, signatories would be given signing authority and everyone would sign the relevant documentation. This live Completion (often called a "closing" in practice) can still take place, but it is now (particularly post Covid-19 pandemic) also common for Completion to take place virtually (i.e., by telephone and e-mail).

If there is a virtual Completion, the documents are generally circulated for signature in advance and the guidance and guidelines in place at the time of Completion on virtual execution must be followed (for example, see the Law Society guidance on virtual execution available at the time of writing).

After Completion, the parties should ensure all original, signed documents should be handed to their solicitors (as original documentation may be needed for post completion matters, although, as noted below, since Covid-19, this is no longer a requirement for stamping the stock transfer forms). Once all filings etc. have been made, the solicitors will return the originals to their clients (together with a transaction bible – see below).

Reason for split exchange and Completion?

As noted above, the most common reason for requiring a gap between exchange and Completion is the need to satisfy conditions precedent. Seller(s) would usually prefer the buyer to be bound to proceed with the transaction by utilising a split exchange and Completion (instead of spending time and money satisfying the conditions and risking the buyer changing their mind before a simultaneous exchange and Completion).

Risks to the buyer with the gap between exchange and Completion

If there is a gap between exchange and Completion, additional clauses must be added to the sale and purchase agreement to both deal with the practicalities involved and also the additional risks the buyer has to consider that are inherent with this gap.

The Seller(s) can be reassured once exchange has taken place, the buyer is bound to purchase the Target/business subject to the conditions precedent being satisfied.

However, this position is not ideal for the buyer, as they are bound to acquire this Target/business in the future but have no control over how it is run or even what may happen in the market (such as a pandemic) from the date of exchange up to the date of Completion. They are bound to pay for and acquire the Target/business at a date in the future but have no control over the entity/business for a period of time prior to the date they will be required to purchase the Target/business – this means that they run the risk of purchasing something very different to what they considered they were purchasing at exchange.

It is also likely that the longer this gap/delay to Completion is, the higher the risks to the buyer – for example, there may be internal issues relating to the Target such as key clients may terminate their arrangements with the Target or key employees leaving, or external issues such as natural disasters (or a pandemic or further lock down that was not anticipated), or the Seller(s) acting outside the ordinary course of business (e.g. by dismissing key employees or taking out new loans). It could even be as simple as the Seller(s) neglecting the business as they know the buyer is bound to complete as soon as the conditions precedent are satisfied.

Additional clauses the buyer may request to deal with a split exchange and Completion are set out below:

Repeating the warranties

The Seller(s) should give the warranties on exchange and then the buyer will ask the Seller(s) to repeat these warranties again at the date of Completion.

There is also likely to be an additional requirement for the Seller(s) to notify the buyer of any breach of warranty (as practically, it will be the Seller(s) who are in still in control of the Target/business during this time period).

The Seller will usually accept the warranty repetition (but will insist on the ability to update the Disclosure Letter at Completion). This will then raise the issue of whether or not the buyer will be able to rescind from the sale and purchase (see below) in relation to any issues relating to breaches of warranty or new disclosures arising in the gap between exchange and Completion.

Right to terminate

The buyer will request that any breach of warranty permits the ability for the buyer to terminate the sale and purchase agreement (i.e., withdraw from the transaction). This is unlikely to be looked on favourably by the Seller(s) as it negates the comfort the Seller(s) has gained from exchanging and binding the buyer to the transaction. The parties may agree that this termination is only possible in the event of a material breach of warranty.

In addition to material breach of warranty, a buyer in a strong position may also wish to include a right to terminate the agreement in the event of a material adverse change ("**MAC**") to the Target or business being sold. If the Seller(s) did agree to this, the risk apportionment "game" discussed in Chapter 9 would come into play again. This is because the risk with a gap between exchange and Completion usually lies with the buyer. By implementing a MAC clause, it moves the risk from the buyer to the Seller(s) in relation to key adverse events occurring in the gap (and these adverse events would need to be carefully negotiated to protect the Seller(s) as much as possible e.g., by limiting it to loss of key clients rather than a general market downturn/impact of a pandemic etc.).

These MAC clauses are currently resisted strongly in the UK (but are much more prevalent in the US). However, since the Covid-19 pandemic, buyers are considering this issue in more detail as the economic impact of the pandemic at the time of writing means the buyer will be keen to ensure the Seller(s) bear the risk of the pandemic having an adverse impact on the Target/business in a gap between exchange and Completion.

Seller actions in the gap

The Seller should be required to run the Target/business in the ordinary course of business during the gap between exchange and Completion. There should also be a list of items that the Seller shall procure the Target/business must not do without the prior written consent of the buyer, for example:

- Dismiss any key employee/director or change their terms of employment;
- Appoint any new directors/make any new hires of directors or key employees;
- Enter into any loan arrangement outside the ordinary course of business;
- Make any capital expenditure above an agreed amount;
- Sell any part of the business or assets (outside the ordinary course of business).

Again, a precedent should be used to ensure all key items are included (such as a requirement to maintain insurance).

Completion

Completion should be managed by the use of a detailed agenda which should include which documents need to be produced/by whom, who the signatories are, which signing authorities are required etc. This should be circulated to all parties in advance so that the Completion can run smoothly without hiccoughs (such as directors who have gone on holiday without executing a power of attorney for someone to sign key documents on their behalf or the failure to hold appropriate meetings to provide authority for signing from corporate parties).

Documents to be provided at exchange

The documents to be provided at exchange are usually fairly simple:

- Sale and purchase agreement (including the Tax Covenant on a share sale)

- Disclosure Letter
- Board minutes of any corporate party to the transaction (providing authority to sign the exchange documents)
- Powers of attorney from any signatory (if required)

In addition, ideally, all of the documents to be provided at Completion (see below) should be in agreed form and produced at exchange for approval.

Documents to be provided at Completion for a share sale

If the transaction is a simultaneous exchange and Completion, the exchange documents will be executed at this point too.

This is only an outline as each deal depends on the facts of the transaction, but it is key to remember that on a share sale, only the shares in the Target are being transferred. The Completion clause in the sale and purchase agreement must be checked as it will set out clearly what needs to be done.

> Example completion clause:
>
> 1.1 At Completion:
>
> (a) the Sellers shall:
>
> (i) deliver or cause to be delivered to the Buyer the items listed in paragraph X of Schedule X;
>
> (ii) procure that a board meeting of the Company is held at which the matters set out in paragraph X Schedule X are carried out; and
>
> (iii) deliver any other documents referred to in this agreement as being required to be delivered by the Sellers at Completion; and
>
> (b) the Buyer shall (subject to the Sellers complying with their obligations in clause X) pay the Purchase Price and deliver to the Sellers:
>
> (i) a signed acknowledgement of the Disclosure Letter; and
>
> (ii) a certified copy of the resolutions of the Buyer's board of directors approving the Transaction and the execution and delivery of the Transaction Documents to be delivered by the Buyer at Completion.

Items listed in the schedule will usually include:

- Stock transfer form for each shareholder;
- Share certificate (or indemnity for lost certificate);
- Any waivers of pre-emption (or any other waivers or consents required to permit buyer to be registered as the new shareholder);
- A power of attorney from each Seller to the buyer to allow the buyer to vote and control any other rights in relation the shares being purchased (this is because the buyer will not be the legal owner of the Target until they are written up in the register of members – this is not done immediately as stamp duty must be paid);
- A board meeting of the Target to approve the registration of the shares and other administrative matters (see completion board meeting contents below);
- The statutory registers of the Target (together with the Target minute book);
- The company seal (if applicable);
- Any certificate of incorporation of the Target;
- Letters of resignation of all officers from all applicable positions including employment position (e.g., directors and secretary if applicable plus auditors);
- Bank statements showing the balances the last Business Day prior to Completion;
- In relation to any properties, all title deeds and any other documentation;
- All securities the Target is a party to together with all documentation relating to the securities (e.g., if they are being released, a deed of release, or consent from the bank/chargeholder to the sale of shares or letter of non-crystallisation in relation to a floating charge);
- Waiver from the Seller(s) of any claims they may have against the Target; and
- Any other documentation relevant to the sale.

As noted in the second sample paragraph above, the main deliverable by the buyer is the payment of the consideration. The method must be agreed in advance as one of the key buyer concerns is they will not wish to pay until the Seller(s) have delivered all their required items (and the Seller(s) will not want to do this until they are happy the buyer has paid. This potentially circular issue can be dealt with in a straightforward manner by the buyer's solicitors holding the consideration in their client account. They can then confirm to the Seller(s)' solicitors that they have the full consideration and can undertake to hold the consideration to the order of the Seller(s) solicitors and instruct the bank to transfer the monies to them the next business day after Completion.

Any instruction to transfer monies must be carried out in accordance with the relevant firm's policy in relation to transfer of client monies in place at the time (for example, the policy may require the instruction is completed by one member of the corporate department, checked by another member of the corporate team and then sent to a different department for separate sign off).

In addition to taking care with instructions to transfer monies, care must also be taken when giving solicitors undertakings – a solicitor must never give an undertaking they cannot fulfil, and there are three key points to take into account in relation to undertakings – these are not just relevant on a corporate transaction but in relation to any undertaking at any time.

Firstly, the SRA Code of Conduct in force at the time of the transaction in relation to solicitors' undertakings must be complied with (e.g., take care with the wording so that you are stating that the solicitor "undertakes to instruct the bank to pay..." and never "undertakes to pay"). The key point with the wording of the undertaking is that it should only cover matters within the solicitor's control (e.g., providing payment instructions to the bank is within your control, ensuring the bank has not gone into insolvency and can send the monies is not).

Secondly, the practical issues must also be carefully dealt with i.e., the buyer's solicitors must ensure they hold the full amount of the monies required, have written instructions from the buyer confirming when the monies can be released/where they should be sent. It must also be agreed what happens to any interest accrued on these monies while being held to the buyer's order.

Finally, the majority of solicitors firms will have a written policy in place relating to when undertakings can be given (and who can sign it). Anyone drafting an undertaking must review the policy in place and ensure it is adhered to.

Completion board meeting of Target

This is a key deliverable and drafts will be circulated and approved by the buyer and the Seller(s) prior to Completion.

As noted above, the buyer will not become the legal owner of the shares in the Target until they are written up in the register of members, therefore the buyer will wish to see this approved by the Target (subject to stamp duty being paid as appropriate) as part of the completion process.

The approval of the transfer of shares is the key element to this meeting but the board meeting will also deal with all the administrative issues inherent in the sale of the Target and there are many precedents available to ensure all of these areas are dealt with e.g. change of officers (resignation of existing directors, appointment of new directors), adopting new articles of association, changing the registered office address, changing the accounting reference date (to ensure the Target's accounting reference date is the same as other group companies within the buyer's group), replacing the bank mandate etc. If there are any subsidiaries within the Target's group, board meetings will also need to take place for each subsidiary company.

It must be noted that any administrative issues approved in the board minutes will usually also have external filing requirements attached and a well organised Completion will have pre-prepared all the appropriate forms for filing so that they may be signed at the time of the Completion board meeting and filed at Companies House shortly afterwards (see post Completion formalities below).

Additional documentation forming part of an asset sale

As noted in Chapter 3, the key element of an asset sale is that each asset agreed to be sold must be transferred to the buyer, and the method of transfer varies depending on the assets being sold. In addition, the sale and purchase agreement and disclosure letter will be required together with items such as waivers of security/certificates of non-crystallisation at noted in relation to a share sale may also be required depending on the facts of the transaction.

Examples of additional Completion deliverables (but each transaction will vary as it depends on the assets in included as part of the transaction) are:

- the assets that are able to be physically delivered to the buyer (which usually includes stock) (and any title documents or certificates that relate to such assets);
- any documents necessary to transfer title in the properties forming part of the transaction (plus title deeds and any other property documentation);
- assignments/novations of contracts, intellectual property and goodwill and any other third-party consents as required;
- certified board minutes/resolution of the Seller authorising the transaction/signatories together with a special resolution of the Seller to change the name if required by the buyer (as discussed in Chapter 9 in relation to acquiring the goodwill); and
- employee documents as noted above.

Post completion formalities

As noted above in relation to the Completion checklist, the post completion formalities will depend on the transaction itself but there are some common items that will be addressed below.

Confirmation of any undertakings

If the buyer's solicitor has provided an undertaking to instruct the bank to pay the monies to the Seller(s)' solicitors, it must ask for a confirmation from the Seller(s)' solicitors in writing that the undertaking has been satisfied.

Stamp duty to be paid on shares

Submitting the stock transfer form(s) for stamping within 30 days of Completion is key. Stamp duty is payable on the transfer of shares (unless the consideration is less than £1,000 or another exemption applies – which is rare on a commercial transaction). Stamp duty is payable at the time of writing at a rate of 0.5% (rounded up to the nearest £5) and it is in the buyer's interest to carry out the stamping (see below).

If the stock transfer form(s) are not stamped, (aside from incurring penalties from HMRC), the Target should refuse to write the buyer up in the register of members.

Since the Covid-19 pandemic, HMRC have now changed the stamping process to permit electronic payment and stamping of stock transfer forms. This means the stock transfer forms are scanned in and emailed to HMRC which is hugely useful in practice and HMRC will respond in writing confirming the stamp duty payment has been received.

Update statutory books (or notify Companies House if the statutory books are kept there)

As noted in the Completion checklist, there will be lots of practical changes taking place within the Target. As well as external filings at Companies House (see forms below), the statutory books of the Target must be updated to reflect these changes i.e., the register of directors, the register of directors' residential addresses, the register of members, the People Having Significant Control register, register of debentures (if applicable) and register of secretaries (if applicable).

In the event that the Target has elected to keep their statutory registers on the public register at Companies House pursuant to the changes implemented under the Small Business, Enterprise and Employment Act 2015, instead of updating their own internal registers, they must notify Companies House of all of the relevant changes on the appropriate forms. These forms are different to the forms required to be filed notifying Companies House to a change of officer etc. (and usually begin with an "E", e.g., EH06 to notify a change to the register of members).

If the buyer has issued shares as part of the consideration, they will also have their own forms to file at Companies House (e.g., Form SH01) plus their internal registers to update to reflect the Seller(s) as shareholders in the buyer and the buyer will be required to issue a share certificate in the buyer to the Seller(s).

External filing obligations

For every change required to an internal register, there is usually an external filing requirement (and associated deadline) to ensure Companies House has the up-to-date details about the Target and its officers. For example, AP01 for new directors, TM01 for resignation of directors, AD01 for change of registered office, AA01 for change to the accounting reference date.

It should be noted that in relation to the PSC forms, the deadlines are slightly different. The internal statutory register must be updated within 14 days of the relevant change to the PSC register (if applicable) and Companies House must be notified on the applicable PSC form 14 days after the statutory register has been updated (so there is a maximum of 28 days to file the relevant PSC forms at Companies House).

In addition, any special resolutions must be filed within 15 days (e.g., changing the name (together with Form NM01 and the appropriate fee) or the articles) together with a print of the new articles of association.

Bibles

After Completion, this is the final step in the transaction. The buyer's solicitor usually takes copies of all of the documents executed as part of the transaction and puts them all together in a file and makes a number of sets of this file.

This file is known as the "**Transaction Bible**". The buyer's solicitor should confirm with each party how many copies of the Transaction Bible they would like and the form they will take (i.e., hard copy or electronic). The Transaction Bible will then be circulated to all parties and acts as a useful reference source for the future (for example, if a particular term of the transaction needs checking or a breach of warranty claim arises).

CHAPTER ELEVEN

EMPLOYMENT CONSIDERATIONS POST-COMPLETION

Now that we have considered all of the elements in a corporate transaction it's important to spend some time reflecting on a client's requirements post Completion. This is often an area that is overlooked by both corporate and employment lawyers and it's essential to think through the issues that clients may have following the deal. In this Chapter, we will explore some key issues that you may need to focus on.

Addressing employee's concerns

A change of ownership can be a very unsettling time for employees. Clearly, through the consultation process employees will have had key integral discussions surrounding any measures that are likely to take place with the transferee. However key employees who are central to the transferee's organisational structure may need some significant support and encouragement. It may be that the transferee needs to negotiate with them directly or require the seller to negotiate on the buyer's behalf. Key employees may also require a significant amount of reassurance from the purchaser as well as requiring a substantial commitment from the transferee. The transferee in turn will want to guarantee that they will remain with them as the new employer after the sale has been completed.

There are number of ways that the transferee may want to address concerns from employees. For example, they may want to negotiate a long fixed term contract or perhaps extend the employee's notice periods, so that the employee has longer term job security. It's also attractive to offer some form of loyalty bonus if the employees remain with the transferee after an agreed date (for example if they remain with the employer for a period of two years, they will receive an additional payment).

Renegotiation of restrictive covenants

Following the due diligence process, it will be clear whether the protection afforded by the restrictive covenants in the employees' contracts is adequate for the transferee's purposes. There are a number of scenarios that the transferee will need to consider here. Sometimes, there are simply no restrictive covenants in the contractual terms, or the covenants do exist but are too wide to be of any benefit. Therefore, the transferee may want to consider amending the contracts of employment for employees to include properly drafted restrictive covenants.

Careful negotiation with the employees needs to take place if the transferee wants to renegotiate new or revised restrictive covenants, as this will involve a change to the employee's terms and conditions. Therefore, as we have seen this will need an ETO reason and employees consent to the change (see Chapter 6).

It's important for any fresh restrictive covenants to be kept up to date if the transferee wants to be able to rely on them. They must be carefully and specifically drafted to reflect the new working arrangements with the transferee. For example, the transferee may want to prevent the employee from entering into from joining a competitive business once the relationship comes to an end.

See also Chapter 9 for the discussion surrounding restrictive covenants from the Seller(s) to the buyer in relation to the business being sold.

Harmonisation

Harmonisation occurs where the transferee wants to place transferred employees on the same terms and conditions as its existing workforce often because it is administratively easier for them. As we have explored in earlier chapters harmonisation is not allowed under TUPE and case law simply does not allow that to happen (see cases including ***Foreningen af Arbejdsledere i Danmark v Daddy's Dance Hall A/S [1988] IRLR 315*** *commonly referred to as* "Daddy's Dance Hall"). So, realistically and in practical terms this will not always be easy or possible to achieve.

There is no express provision in TUPE for harmonisation, and the government's guidance on TUPE makes it clear that the government did not include such provision as it considers it not be permissible given CJEU case law. The EAT has also confirmed this as the position (see the case of ***London Metropolitan University v Sackur (UKEAT/014/06)***).

Agreement

The obvious way to make variations is to obtain employees agreement to those changes. However, clients should still be advised that there is a risk that the employee could "cherry pick" between new and old terms if they do so, and the need to balance and manage that risk carefully (see ***Regent Security Services Ltd v Power [2007] EWCA Civ 1188).***

The Power decision has also been incorporated into the BEIS guidance on this point which states: *"Changes to terms and conditions agreed by the parties which are entirely positive are not prevented by the Regulations."*

Another solution is to end the old contractual terms under a settlement agreement and to re-engage on fresh terms and conditions post transfer. The dismissing employer would have to dismiss on some other substantial reasons grounds. Both parties need to be advised very carefully as this would risk an automatic unfair dismissal related to the transfer. In which case a very carefully drafted settlement agreement will be required to eliminate this risk.

What does TUPE say about changes in working conditions?

As we have seen Regulation 4 provides that any purported variation to a transferring employee's employment contract is void if the sole or principal reason for the variation is the transfer (Regulation 4(4)).

However, Regulation 4(4) does not prevent contractual variation if:

(1) the sole or principal reason for the variation is an economic, technical or organisational reason ("ETO reason") entailing changes in the workforce, provided that the employer and employee agree the variation (Regulation 4(5); or

(2) the terms of the contract permit the employer to make such a variation (Regulation 4(5)(b)).

Clearly, the transferee also needs to be mindful of Regulation 4(9) – that an employee may treat the contract as terminated by the employer on any substantial change in working conditions to his material detriment. Regulation 4(11) also confirms that the employee retains the right to claim normal constructive dismissal in response to a fundamental breach of their contract of employment by the employer.

The parties need to receive careful advice on both of these aspects of the TUPE Regulations in order to manage and balance the risk.

S188 Trade Union and Labour Relations Consolidation Act 1992

The transferee needs to be aware that dismissal and re-engagement of 20 or more employees will also trigger the obligation to collectively consult under section 188 **of Trade Union and Labour Relations Consolidation Act 1992 ("TULRCA")**.

Also, because the definition of redundancy under TULRCA is wider than under the Employment Rights Act 1996 it includes a situation where an employer changes terms and conditions through dismissal and then re-engagement. The stakes are high. If clients do not want to go through the obligations under section 188 and employees, or unions on the employee's behalf, pursue claims the remedy is a Protective Award of up to 90 days pay for each affected employee. Again, clearly this is for the parties to manage and balance their risk and weighing up the overall value of the commercial transaction.

GLOSSARY OF TERMS

Term	Summary
Business sale	See TOGC below.
CA 2006	Companies Act 2006.
Completion	When all of the formalities are concluded in relation to the acquisition.
Conditions precedent	Conditions set out in the sale and purchase agreement that are required to be satisfied after Exchange (with completion conditional upon their satisfaction).
Constructive dismissal	When an employee resigns and feels that they have no option but to do so because of the employer's unreasonable behaviour.
ETO	Economic, technical or organisational reason entailing changes in the workforce.
ERA 1996	Employment Rights Act 1996.
Exchange	The moment where the sale and purchase agreement is executed by both parties (and the disclosure letter is delivered).
Garden leave	A contractual clause preventing an employee from attending work during their notice period.
Heads of Terms	A summary of the basic terms of the transaction.

PILON	Pay in lieu of notice.
Restrictive covenants	Clauses preventing an employee from doing certain things after the employment relationship has ended. (e.g., competing with the ex-employer, or taking clients with them on leaving).
SAIL	Single Alternative Inspection Location.
Single Alternative Inspection Location	Location of the statutory registers of the Target (if they are not kept at the registered office).
Summary dismissal	The dismissal of an employee without notice or pay in lieu of notice.
Target	In a share sale, this is the company that is the subject of the share sale.
TOGC	Transfer of a Going Concern.
Transfer of a Going Concern	The sale and purchase of an operating business including all of the elements necessary to keep it operating after the sale.
TUPE	Transfer of Undertakings (Protection of Employment) Regulations 2006.
Unfair dismissal	Statutory right not to be unfairly dismissed under the Employment Rights Act 1996.
Wrongful dismissal	When an employee has been dismissed in breach of their employment contract.

'Covid-19, Homeworking and the Law – The Essential Guide to Employment and GDPR Issues' by Forbes Solicitors
'Covid-19, Force Majeure and Frustration of Contracts – The Essential Guide' by Keith Markham
'Covid-19 and Criminal Law – The Essential Guide' by Ramya Nagesh
'Covid-19 and Family Law in England and Wales – The Essential Guide' by Safda Mahmood
'A Practical Guide to the Law of Unlawful Eviction and Harassment – 2nd Edition' by Stephanie Lovegrove
'Covid-19, Residential Property, Equity Release and Enfranchisement – The Essential Guide' by Paul Sams and Louise Uphill
'Covid-19, Brexit and the Law of Commercial Leases – The Essential Guide' by Mark Shelton
'A Practical Guide to Costs in Personal Injury Claims – 2nd Edition' by Matthew Hoe
'A Practical Guide to the General Data Protection Regulation (GDPR) – 2nd Edition' by Keith Markham
'Ellis on Credit Hire – Sixth Edition' by Aidan Ellis & Tim Kevan
'A Practical Guide to Working with Litigants in Person and McKenzie Friends in Family Cases' by Stuart Barlow
'Protecting Unregistered Brands: A Practical Guide to the Law of Passing Off' by Lorna Brazell
'A Practical Guide to Secondary Liability and Joint Enterprise Post-Jogee' by Joanne Cecil & James Mehigan
'A Practical Guide to the Pre-Action RTA Claims Protocol for Personal Injury Lawyers' by Antonia Ford
'A Practical Guide to Neighbour Disputes and the Law' by Alexander Walsh
'A Practical Guide to Forfeiture of Leases' by Mark Shelton
'A Practical Guide to Coercive Control for Legal Practitioners and Victims' by Rachel Horman

'A Practical Guide to Rights Over Airspace and Subsoil' by Daniel Gatty
'Tackling Disclosure in the Criminal Courts – A Practitioner's Guide' by Narita Bahra QC & Don Ramble
'A Practical Guide to the Law of Driverless Cars – Second Edition' by Alex Glassbrook, Emma Northey & Scarlett Milligan
'A Practical Guide to TOLATA Claims' by Greg Williams
'Artificial Intelligence – The Practical Legal Issues' by John Buyers
'A Practical Guide to the Law of Prescription in Scotland' by Andrew Foyle
'A Practical Guide to the Construction and Rectification of Wills and Trust Instruments' by Edward Hewitt
'A Practical Guide to the Law of Bullying and Harassment in the Workplace' by Philip Hyland
'How to Be a Freelance Solicitor: A Practical Guide to the SRA-Regulated Freelance Solicitor Model' by Paul Bennett
'A Practical Guide to Prison Injury Claims' by Malcolm Johnson
'A Practical Guide to the Small Claims Track' by Dominic Bright
'A Practical Guide to Advising Clients at the Police Station' by Colin Stephen McKeown-Beaumont
'A Practical Guide to Antisocial Behaviour Injunctions' by Iain Wightwick
'Practical Mediation: A Guide for Mediators, Advocates, Advisers, Lawyers, and Students in Civil, Commercial, Business, Property, Workplace, and Employment Cases' by Jonathan Dingle with John Sephton
'The Mini-Pupillage Workbook' by David Boyle
'A Practical Guide to Crofting Law' by Brian Inkster
'A Practical Guide to Spousal Maintenance' by Liz Cowell
'A Practical Guide to the Law of Domain Names and Cybersquatting' by Andrew Clemson
'A Practical Guide to the Law of Gender Pay Gap Reporting' by Harini Iyengar

'A Practical Guide to the Rights of Grandparents in Children Proceedings' by Stuart Barlow
'NHS Whistleblowing and the Law' by Joseph England
'Employment Law and the Gig Economy' by Nigel Mackay & Annie Powell
'A Practical Guide to Noise Induced Hearing Loss (NIHL) Claims' by Andrew Mckie, Ian Skeate, Gareth McAloon
'An Introduction to Beauty Negligence Claims – A Practical Guide for the Personal Injury Practitioner' by Greg Almond
'Intercompany Agreements for Transfer Pricing Compliance' by Paul Sutton
'Zen and the Art of Mediation' by Martin Plowman
'A Practical Guide to the SRA Principles, Individual and Law Firm Codes of Conduct 2019 – What Every Law Firm Needs to Know' by Paul Bennett
'A Practical Guide to Adoption for Family Lawyers' by Graham Pegg
'A Practical Guide to Industrial Disease Claims' by Andrew Mckie & Ian Skeate
'A Practical Guide to Redundancy' by Philip Hyland
'A Practical Guide to Vicarious Liability' by Mariel Irvine
'A Practical Guide to Applications for Landlord's Consent and Variation of Leases' by Mark Shelton
'A Practical Guide to Relief from Sanctions Post-Mitchell and Denton' by Peter Causton
'A Practical Guide to Equity Release for Advisors' by Paul Sams
'A Practical Guide to the Law Relating to Food' by Ian Thomas
'A Practical Guide to Financial Services Claims' by Chris Hegarty
'The Law of Houses in Multiple Occupation: A Practical Guide to HMO Proceedings' by Julian Hunt
'A Practical Guide to Unlawful Eviction and Harassment' by Stephanie Lovegrove
'Occupiers, Highways and Defective Premises Claims: A Practical Guide Post-Jackson – 2nd Edition' by Andrew Mckie

www.ingramcontent.com/pod-product-compliance
Lightning Source LLC
LaVergne TN
LVHW022056200926
848481LV00003B/941